The Official

MARSHALL'S HANDCOLORING GUIDE & GALLERY

THE TOOLS & TECHNIQUES
of
HANDCOLORING
USING MARSHALL'S MATERIALS

By

GRACE & GEORGE SCHAUB

© 2000 John G. Marshall Company
A Division of Brandess-Kalt-Aetna Group, Inc.

First Printing: 1994
Published by: G&G Schaub
Art Director: Grace Schaub

Editorial Advisor: Muriel Brandess
Typesetting, Layout by: American Graphics
Printed by: Action Printing

Cover photograph © Richard Prehn

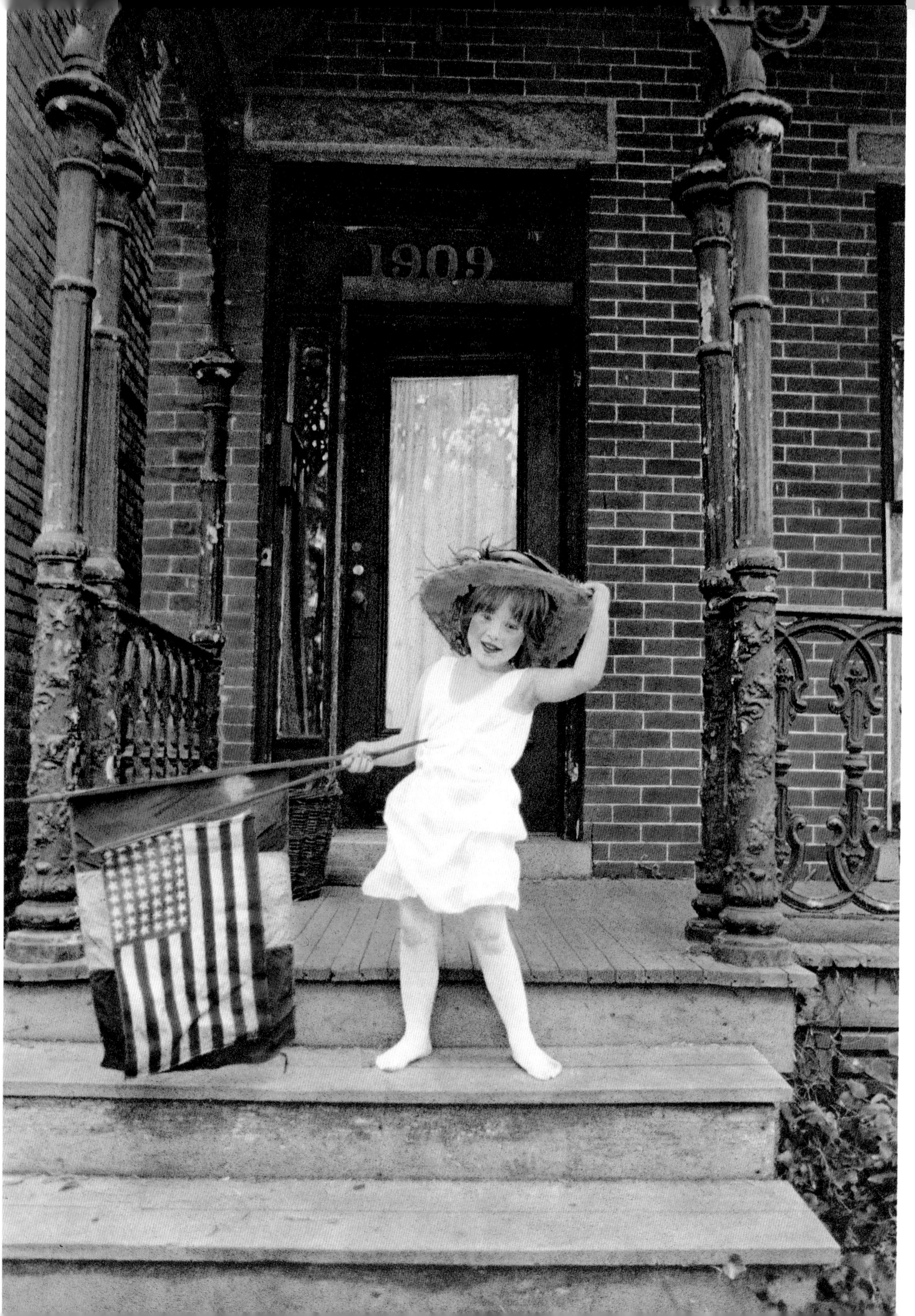
1909

CONTENTS

INTRODUCTION

Welcome to the world of handcoloring. Ever since the invention of photography, handcoloring has been both a pragmatic way of adding color to monochrome images, and an art form that has appealed to a broad range of photographers and other visual artists. And, when color photography and other color media such as color copies and computer-generated thermal prints grew, it became a way of adding an extra touch of color, or altering and correcting the color that appeared on the original image.

Handcoloring offers both freedom of expression and a hands-on feeling of involvement in working with images. It is a very user-friendly medium, allowing application, correction and fine-tuning to be accomplished with ease. It allows for both naturalistic and highly-imaginative renditions, and gives users an easy way to blend and mix colors. It is a "what-you-see-is-what-you-get" medium, one that requires a very small investment yet yields rich rewards. True, there are colorizing programs for computer-based imagery, yet the time, effort and equipment required, and the quality of the media on which the work is output, often limits the photographer/artist.

Handcoloring has risen in popularity of late, due to its "rediscovery" by a new generation of photographers, and to its incorporation in a wide range of commercial applications. There is a visual "feel" to the medium that is unique, one that lends itself to experimentation and encourages individual interpretations of imagery.

The purpose of this guide is to give you an introduction to, and a working familiarity with the creative materials available from the John G. Marshall Company. Throughout this guide, practical examples and proven methods of working will be discussed. As with any medium, and with any handbook, the true limits of expression can only be explored by the individual working with the materials. The idea here is to give you the tools, some advice, and to encourage you to experiment with your own images and imagination. That's the beauty of these materials—they do not limit the sense of color and design of the person working with them.

The book is organized so that you can either read it all the way through and then begin to work, or use it as an occasional reference guide when you have a specific project in mind. Tips, charts and quick-reference sections are included.

The first section takes a look at the role handcoloring has played in photographic history, and how the John G. Marshall Manufacturing Company has played its part. Early examples of handcoloring include both commercial imagery and personal portraiture. Indeed, any family album or picture collection that dates back more than forty years probably contains a number of hand-colored portraits and hand-colored postcards and souvenirs.

The materials guide section follows, and is a catalog of the photo oils, pencils, retouch colors and other materials used in coloring and retouching in the Marshall's line, along with some brief practical tips on their use. The entire range of Marshall products offers sprays, brushes and other items used in the craft. Included are descriptions of the various kits offered by the company.

The applications section is a basic primer on working methods, and contains information you will find useful in your work, such as advice on how to apply colors, the use of various papers, color schemes and other matters that will enhance your work with the materials. Along with this practical information are tips that can help you achieve certain special effects. Numerous charts and illustrations are provided.

The gallery section is a showcase of work done by artists/photographers, and displays both the diversity of work and the flexibility of the materials. It also serves as a guide to the nuances of the materials, and how each artist uses them in their work. A short biography of the artist and their intent, plus insider's information on how they achieved certain effects accompanies the illustrations.

This book has been created to serve as a companion to your handcoloring work and as an inspiration that will help you explore the possibilities. We hope that it serves you well, and that it provides the information you need.

The production of this guide would not have been possible without the enthusiastic cooperation of the many artists whose work appears in these pages. The energy and excitement with which they approach the work is part of what makes handcoloring such a fascinating art form.

In addition, the true impetus behind this guide has been provided by Muriel Brandess and the people of the Brandess/Kalt/Aetna Group. Muriel is rightly acknowledged by many of those involved with handcoloring as the person who is most responsible for its continued success and growth. This book is dedicated to her.

Handcoloring and Photography

Ever since the invention of photography, hand-coloring, in one form or another, has been a companion art. The most popular use of the medium had been in the colorizing of mono-chrome portraiture, a practice that compensated for the lack of color films. With the invention of photography, miniaturist painters were virtually put out of work, and many turned to coloring photographs as freelancers or as employees of photo studios. Large-scale handcoloring of portraits continued well into the 1950's.

Handcoloring was not limited to portraiture. Landscape, still life and nature photography all benefited from handcoloring; indeed, it is said that a surprising number of painters used the photograph as a form of sketch, and then applied oils over the print to create the final painting.

Historians note that handcoloring arrived with the invention of photography itself in 1839.

The first known attempts were by assistants of W.H. Fox Talbot, the Englishman credited with perfecting the paper negative process. As the final prints were produced on a matte surface paper, the application of watercolors and trans-parent oil paints to add the "colors of nature" were a simple matter.

The same demand arose for adding color to the daguerrotype; however, as this was an image affixed to a metal plate, adding color was no simple matter. The daugerrotype, as beautiful as it was in detail, was a "cold" medium for portraits. The technique involved color powders which were "fixed" with various chemicals or, in some instances, by the painter's breath. Colors were also added to the underside of the protective glass plate. Detailed coloring of the image was difficult, at best.

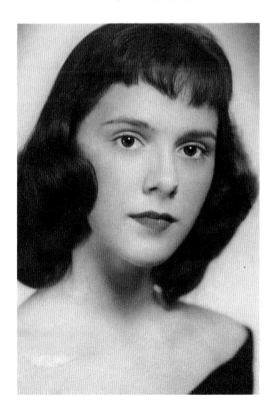 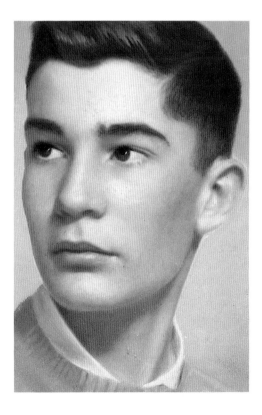

Handcoloring of studio portraits was one of the main uses of the craft. While done to a lesser extent today, they are still in demand by discriminating clients. These high school yearbook portraits of the authors were handcolored by studio artists in the early 1960's.

NEW MEDIUMS

As the development of various photographic mediums progressed, so did handcoloring. In 1851, when Frederick Scott Archer introduced the collodion process—an image affixed to a glass plate—transparent oil colors and dry powders dissolved in alcohol were used to add color. Similarly, lantern slides were also colorized.

The albumen process (which was an emulsion coated on the surface with a thin film of egg white) soon replaced Talbot's salted paper process. However, as this was a smooth, glossy surface, colors were sometimes difficult to affix. The answer was using a wetting agent to help with color absorbency.

One of the most fascinating manifestations of handcoloring was the crystoleum. An albumen print was placed face down inside a curved glass, and affixed with paste. When the print dried, the paper backing was sanded away, leaving a very thin backing and the image layer. To help transparency, the print was rubbed with wax or oil. Color was then added from the back of the print. The crystoleum was available up to the beginning of World War I.

Bromide papers arrived in the 1870's, and with them came a booming trade in the coloring of portraits and the carte de visite, postcard-size photo calling cards that were all the rage. Most Victorian-era studios offered handcoloring as a regular part of their trade, and employed full-time artists for this service.

HANDCOLORING ON CANVAS

As early as 1859, methods were devised for enlarging photographs on canvas, or a canvas-like paper stock, so that artists could then add color to the image. Known as "photo painting", the technique was used extensively by portraitists and landscape photographers. Established painters often resented this technique, and considered it an inferior art form. There are many recorded debates, with high ideals expressed about the dangers to "pure" art. However, numerous instances are also recorded about photo painting making its way into the hallowed halls of the art academy.

In his landmark book, "Art and Photography", Aaron Scharf recounts an article published in a journal known as the "Photographic News" in 1861.

"Critical of the exclusion of photographs from the (English) Royal Academy and other exhibitions, especially since painters who were known to work over faint photographic images were admitted, the Photographic News quoted with relish an 'indisputable authority' who reported that not only had the Royal Academy unknowingly accepted a 'coloured photograph' for their exhibition but that it was 'hung on the line' (in the exhibit.)" Scharf goes on to say, "By about 1860 the practice of 'High Art' photography had noticeably increased; its techniques, 'like the painter's brush', included a considerable variety of retouching methods."

Handcoloring was also used for display prints, and became decoration for the home. A number of photographers, with Wallace Nutting being among the best known today, organized cottage industries composed of painters who applied color over his prints. The Nutting work has its stenciled quality, but additional flourishes of color and highlights separated them from much of the work done on similar decorative prints. The Nutting prints have become collectible, and have moved from country flea market stalls and garage sales into galleries and antique shops today.

THE POSTCARD BOOM

Handcoloring also became used extensively in the production of postcards and souvenirs. The final colors were generally applied with a form of silk screening, with stencils cut for each block or pattern of color on the cards. The colors used were certainly not limited to those found in the real world, and some of the colorists created fantastic visions of the various destinations. The color combinations ranged from gaudy to surreal, although some of the artists did strive for as naturalistic a rendition as possible.

Once color photography for the masses emerged in the 1950's, the use of handcoloring went into a period of decline, and was practiced mostly by portrait studios and their associated artists as a special service to select clients. While those who have remained dedicated to handcoloring throughout those years built a solid and loyal clientele, most photographers and artists paid more attention to color film and printing than they did to handcoloring. Labs offered laminating or mounting services that bound conventional color paper to canvas-backed boards, thus giving the look of a painting to a color print.

Handcoloring has always been allied with photography. This carte de visite of a soldier (upper left) was photographed and colored , probably by the resident studio artist, in the 1870s. Handcolored souvenir postcards (above) often sported surreal colors, applied to the original then run off on mass printing presses. Wallace Nutting's workshops (left) created bucolic hand-colored orginals that were sold as wall decor, and are now collectible. (All images, collection of the authors.)

REDISCOVERY

The late 1960's saw the reappearance of handcoloring as an art form. People were exploring new realities and new forms of expression. Coupled with imaginative images, handcoloring allowed them to add whatever colors and forms they desired to the print. While some artists painted "within the lines", others used handcoloring as part of a collage approach to the photographic image, or applied pencils and paints in ways that transformed the original image to an entirely new scene.

© Prehn

As with many art forms, handcoloring was co-opted into the commercial world, and many of the techniques and approaches of the sixties became part of the mainstream advertising and fashion photography of the seventies and eighties. Today, handcoloring rests comfortably in both the commercial and the "fine art" photography realms. Indeed, the renaissance of black-and-white imagery in all aspects of photography has meant a similar growth in the use and practice of handcoloring.

Today, the broad-based appeal of handcoloring has meant that it is commonly seen in both the fine art portfolio and the commercial "book."

There are those who use it as a way of adding their own special "take" on a particular scene, and those who work in a decidedly naturalistic fashion. A scan through the magazine racks shows the diversity of the art. In one magazine it may be used for a fashion spread—in another it may be used in the Lifestyle section to colorize a still life of food. Travel magazines may have destination pieces using the medium, while interviews may use handcolored portraits for illustration.

In short, handcoloring has become a widely accepted medium for illustrative photography, and is certainly to be considered one of the tools of the photographic trade.

While the commercial purposes of the craft are obvious, there is also the pure pleasure of working in the medium. Once begun, the ease of use, and the freedom of expression becomes apparent. Application, correction and highlighting requires no more than a few strokes of the hand, and becomes immediately appealing to any visual artist.

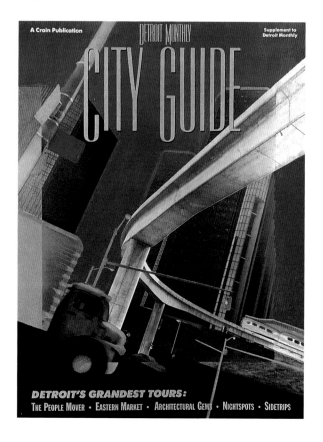

Image: © Rita Dibert; Cover © Crain Communications, Inc.

THE JOHN G. MARSHALL COMPANY
AND BRANDESS/KALT/AETNA GROUP

Throughout the history of the medium, various companies produced kits and individual color sets specifically designed for handcoloring photographs. In the 1930's, along with Marshall, companies such as Eastman Kodak, Peerless, and Roehrig-Bielenberg offered both regular and extra-strong colors, premium cotton for application, tray palettes and various application devices in kits marketed through both art supply and specialty photo stores.

Many photographic schools offered courses in handcoloring utilizing the colors from Marshall. The National Photo Coloring School, based in Chicago, offered a study-by-mail course with

various lessons, prints for coloring and critiques by instructors. These were offered to both photo studios and freelance handcolorists. The craft was touted as an excellent source of extra income for freelancers who would "find photo studios among your best customers." A sample lesson included: "Color combinations to achieve harmony; money-making ideas; suggestions and ideas for novelties; coloring pictures for parchment lamp shades; and how to bring out sunlight."

Lucile Robertson, a former vp of John G. Marshall Co. wrote extensively on the subject— including books and magazine articles—and was once hailed as the "most richly qualified authority on photo oil coloring in America." During the Second World War, she trained hundreds of teachers in handcoloring for occupational therapy

programs in service and veteran hospitals, and later did the same work for Volunteer Service Photographers, Inc. (and later through Rehabilitation through Photography—RTP.)

The John G. Marshall Company was founded in 1919, and was primarily a chemical-supply company that offered a variety of products marketed through photo specialty stores. Early items included a "fine-grain" liquid developer selling for $1.25 a quart; Rodinal for $2.00 a quart; powdered paper developers for 50 cents; and powder to make 5 quarts of fixer for 40 cents. In addition, they offered Marshall's Flares, pyrotechnic torches that "burn with great brilliancy, and can be used for night and cave photography." However, the company brochure warned, "Their use indoors is not advised because of the smoke they emit."

Once introduced, Marshall's Photo Oils became a major calling card for the company. A vital part of their marketing was the continual production of a wide range of books, brochures and how-to-color literature. The company produced sets of black-and-white prints of both photographs and line-drawings with detailed instructions on how to color in between the lines. The Marshall's pixie, a leprachaun-like character with curved-toe shoes and an "M" on its chest, became a well-known company mascot.

The company was family-owned, and was staffed by loyal employees. Eventually, the photo chemistry side of the business declined, and the photo oils and pencils became their main line of business. However, through the years the business lessened, and there was great concern that the last-remaining supply of photo oils and pencils would disappear. The author can remember that time, when stocks of colors

This Marshall's Photo Oil Color advertisement appeared in a 1945 issue of Popular Photography. The accompanying picture was used to promote a handcoloring contest that offered a $500 War Bond prize to the winner. (Picture, upper left, courtesy Curtice Taylor.)

became low or non-existent, and fewer and fewer dealers carried the materials.

Happily, in the early 1980's, Charles and Muriel Brandess of Brandess Corporation became aware of the company's changing fortunes, and purchased the distribution and manufacturing facilities of the then Brooklyn, New York-based firm. The Brandess Company, which has since become Brandess/Kalt/Aetna Group, has been a true advocate of the line, and has supported it fully.

They have donated products to worthy organizations such as Rehabilitation Through Photography, Inc.. This non-profit agency's good works include sponsoring an annual Photo Oil competition named for its founder, Lucile Robertson Marshall. Through this foundation, the Marshall Photo Oil Company is able to encourage

the art and craft of handcoloring by donation of materials for use in their ongoing classes for the physically and emotionally handicapped of all ages, disadvantaged youth, senior citizens, psychiatric patients, AIDS patients, substance abusers in recovery and nursing home residents.

The Marshall Company further encourages the exploration of handcoloring through demonstrations, workshops and professional photographic organizations. Muriel Brandess has truly been a champion of handcoloring and the Marshall's line.

The publication of this guide marks the 75th Anniversary of the Marshall's Company. It is done in respect and admiration of all the books and articles that have preceded it, and hopefully will serve as a text for future generations of handcolorists.

Materials Guide

TRANSPARENT PHOTO OILS

The transparent photo oils, available in 2-inch and 4-inch tubes, are the heart of the the Marshall's painting system. These specially-formulated oils are the standards of the industry, and have been recognized the world over for their quality and consistency. The oils can be purchased individually or in sets, depending upon your needs.

There are two types of oils-Regular and Extra-Strong. The Regular colors are for most needs, and are used for portraits, naturalistic landscapes and other pictorial purposes. The Extra-Strong Colors are highly concentrated, and are used when brilliant tones are desired. They can also be used to impart a surrealistic element to scenes, or for abstract studies. The two types of oils may be mixed for even more color choices.

In addition to the Oils, the Marshall's System is composed of various coloring aids. These include P.M. Solution, Extender, Marlene, Drier and Duolac. Some or all of these aids are contained in the various Marshall's Kits, or can be purchased separately.

MARSHALL'S PHOTO PENCIL SETS

Many colorists find that Marshall's Photo Pencil Sets are a perfect complement to Marshall's Photo Oils; indeed, the colors of the pencils are matched to the photo oils, and are often used for detail work. However, many artists also use the pencils as the sole source of color on the print. Whether worked individually or in combination with oils, the fine controls these pencils afford make them ideal for a wide range of subject matter and effects.

MARSHALL'S PHOTO OILS AND PENCIL SETS

The extensive line of colors in Photo Oils and Pencils allows you to create images with a dazzling array of possibilities. In addition, the ability to mix oils means that virtually any color you desire can be created. This listing shows the colors that are available, the sizes in which they are available and those colors that come in both Regular and Extra-Strong formulations. See color chart on page 17.

Color	Regular 2"	Regular 4"	Extra Strong 2"	Extra Strong 4"	Pencils
Air Force Blue	✓	✓			
Army Green	✓	✓			
Background Aqua	✓	✓			
Background Tan	✓	✓			
Basic Flesh	✓	✓			✓
Basic Flesh Shadow	✓	✓			
Burnt Sienna	✓	✓			
Blue Violet					✓
Cadmium Orange	✓	✓	✓	✓	✓
Cadmium Yellow	✓	✓	✓	✓	✓
Cadmium Yellow Deep	✓	✓	✓	✓	✓
Caribbean Green					✓
Carmine	✓	✓	✓	✓	
Cerise	✓	✓			
Cheek	✓	✓			✓
Chinese Blue	✓	✓	✓	✓	
Cobalt Violet	✓	✓	✓	✓	✓

A ✓ indicates availability. A blank space indicates that the color is not available in certain sizes and/or formulations.

Color	Regular		Extra Strong		Pencils
	2"	4"	2"	4"	
Comb. Flesh Shadow	✓	✓			
Electric Blue					✓
Flesh	✓	✓			
Flesh No. 2	✓	✓			
Flesh No. 3	✓	✓			
Gold					✓
Grayed Background Blue	✓	✓			
Grayed Background Green	✓	✓			
Ivory Black	✓	✓	✓	✓	✓
Khaki	✓	✓			
Lemon Yellow					✓
Lip	✓	✓			
Lipstick Red	✓	✓			✓
Mauve					✓
Navy Blue	✓	✓			✓
Neutral Tint	✓	✓			
Orchid	✓				
Oxide Green	✓	✓	✓	✓	✓
Paynes Gray	✓	✓	✓	✓	
Periwinkle Blue					✓
Pumpkin					✓
Raw Sienna	✓	✓	✓	✓	✓
Sepia	✓	✓	✓	✓	✓
Serge Blue	✓	✓			
Silver					✓
Sky Blue	✓	✓			✓
Teal Blue					✓
Terra Cotta					✓
Titanium White	✓	✓			✓
Tree Green	✓	✓	✓	✓	✓
Ultra Blue	✓	✓	✓	✓	✓
Vermilion	✓	✓	✓	✓	
Verona Brown	✓	✓	✓	✓	✓
Viridian	✓	✓	✓	✓	✓
Warm Pink					✓

A ✓ indicates availability. A blank space indicates that the color is not available in certain sizes and/or formulations.

MARSHALL'S PHOTO OILS KITS

These kits have been put together to appeal to both the beginning and advanced handcolorist. As you work from these kits, you may find that you use certain colors more than others. For example, those who work in landscapes may use more Raw Sienna, Sepia and Tree Green than Lipstick Red or Cobalt Violet Extra Strong. Or, those who prefer doing handcolored portraits will be going through their Lip, Flesh No. 2 and Basic Flesh Shadow faster than they will Viridian, Oxide Green or Air Force Blue. All the colors contained in the kits can also be purchased separately.

The Introductory Set serves a beginner's needs. It contains five colors in 2-inch tubes and a bottle of P.M. Solution. While the color selection is limited, colors can be mixed to create many more options for your handcoloring needs.

The Learn to Color Set contains nine assorted Photo Oil colors in 2-inch tubes, a bottle of P.M. Solution, plus a tube of Extender.

The Hobby Oil Set contains 15 2-inch tubes of oil colors, a 4-inch tube of Extender, a bottle of P.M. Solution, a mixing palette, 100% pure cotton and a bottle of Marlene.

For those who wish to have a more extensive set of colors, the Advanced Oil Set may be selected. This contains 20 2-inch tubes of assorted colors, a tube of Extender, a bottle of Marlene, a bottle of P.M. Solution, a 1-ounce bottle of Duolac and a 4-inch tube of Drier, plus 100% pure cotton.

For the dedicated handcolorist. The Master Oil Set contains all of the Marshall's coloring aids (P.M. Solution, Extender, Marlene, Duolac and Drier), 100% pure cotton and 46 2-inch tubes of color. This gives you virtually every color available in the Marshall's spectrum of oils.

MARSHALL'S PHOTO PENCIL SETS

The Starter Pencil Set contains nine assorted colors, 100% pure cotton and a bottle of P.M. Solution. Treat prints with a very light coat of P.M. Solution prior to working with pencils. If used in combination with oils, use of P.M. Solution is unnecessary.

The Advanced Pencil Set contains 14 assorted colors, along with a bottle of P.M. Solution and 100% pure cotton. Pencils are also available individually.

The Tropical Pencil Set contains 14 assorted pencils including exciting new colors: electric blue, terra cotta, lemon yellow, olive green, blue violet, carmine pink, flesh, pumpkin, Caribbean green, periwinkle blue, warm pink, silver and gold, 1/2 oz. bottle of P.M. Solution, skewers, cotton and instructions.

MARSHALL'S COMBINATION SETS

Learn to Color with Photos Set contains 9 assorted 1/2 x 2" oil color tubes, 1/2 x 2" tube of Extender, 1 oz. bottle of P.M. Solution, skewers, cotton and instructions. Also includes one three-picture Photo Set.

Portrait Set contains 10 assorted 1/2 x 2" oil color tubes, 6 photo pencils, a 1/2 x 2" tube of Extender, eraser, skewers, cotton and "how to" instructions for coloring portraits.

Click-N-Color Camera Set - contains everything you need to make your own colorful creations. The set contains a single use 35mm camera with black & white film and built-in flash, 5 assorted 1/2" x 2" oil color tubes, 6 photo pencils, vinyl eraser, cotton and picks.

Pencil and Oil Activity Set contains one professional 8" x 10" black and white photograph, 5 assorted 1/2 x 2" oil color tubes, 6 assorted photo coloring pencils, 1/2 oz. bottle of P.M. Solution, skewers, cotton an Eberhard Faber vinyl eraser and instructions.

TRANSPARENT PHOTO COLOR OIL CHART

Sky Blue | Air Force Blue | Navy Blue
Chinese Blue | Chinese Blue extra strong | Basic Flesh
Ultra Blue | Ultra Blue extra strong | Basic Flesh Shadow
Paynes Gray | Paynes Gray extra strong | Flesh
Lip | Lipstick Red | Flesh No. 2
Cerise | Cheek | Flesh No. 3
Vermilion | Vermilion extra strong | Comb. Fl. Shadow

Serge Blue | Carmine | Carmine extra strong
Army Green | Cobalt Violet | Cobalt Violet extra strong
Khaki | Cadmium Yellow | Cadmium Yellow extra strong
Neutral Tint | Cadmium yellow deep | Cadmium Yellow Deep extra strong
Cadmium Orange | Cadmium Orange extra strong

Raw Sienna | Raw Sienna extra strong | Grayed Bkgd. Blue
Verona Brown | Verona Brown extra strong | Grayed Bkgd. Green
Sepia | Sepia extra strong | Burnt Sienna
Oxide Green | Oxide Green extra strong | Ivory Black
Tree Green | Tree Green extra strong | Ivory Black extra strong
Viridian | Viridian extra strong | Opaque / Titanium White

Transparent Photo Oil
Color Chart
Select from these 53 permanent Transparent Colors
Actual colors may vary slightly from this printed chart.

Extra Strong Colors of the line, add vividness. They have the effect of opaque colors without obscuring the photographic image.

MARSHALL'S SPOT-ALL LIQUIDS

Marshall also offers a full line of spotting colors, available in sets, for black-and-white prints and negatives. The colors can be used on all types of papers, including RC. Some colors may be used on prints right out of the dropper-type bottle. However, the image color of monochrome prints may vary from green-black to blue-black, depending upon the paper and developer used, and any toning or after-treatment the print may receive. Thus, you may find it necessary to combine colors to achieve the best result. The variety of Spot-All Liquids, and the variations that can be obtained by mixing those colors, means that you can match any image color on any monochrome paper, whether it be toned or untoned. In addition, these Spot-All Liquids may be used to spot prints prior to handcoloring or tinting, and will not smear or rub off during the color application.

Spot-All Liquids are available in kit form. Set 3B contains blue/black, for cold-tone papers, selenium/brown, for selenium-toned prints, and neutral black, for most neutral-tone papers. Set 6BT (shown below) contains all the dyes found in Set 3B, plus specialty colors including sepia brown, brown tone and olive brown (for chlorobromide papers).

MARSHALL'S PHOTO RETOUCH COLORS

Marshall's Photo Retouch Colors are made specifically for photographic media, including color prints, black-and-white prints and slides. In addition, they can be applied to many types of non-photographic imaging media, including laser color copy paper, thermal color paper (generated from computer-imaging systems) and virtually any type of material that will absorb dye. In general, and for the most control, Marshall's Liquid Retouch Colors should be applied with a brush.

The colors are all self-blending, which means they can be applied over one another until the desired color or effect is achieved. In addition, the colors are concentrated, so that some dilution may be required, although color can also be used directly from the bottle.

The colors fall into three basic categories-Primary, Basic and Bright. The Primary Colors are matched to the dyes found in color papers, and are generally used for "spotting" the dust and lint defects that are too often a part of print finishing. They may also be used when vivid colors are desired. The Basic Colors are used for overall color correction, and are matched to the direct colors that appear in color prints, rather than for spotting. For example, you might use a Basic Color to alter the color of a highlight, or to add some richness to portions of a sky. The Bright Colors are used for adding accents of colors to flowers, bright fabrics or for bringing vivid colors to any subject within the scene.

Marshall's Photo Retouch Colors are available in kit form with eight colors in each kit. These versatile dyes can be used for retouching and enhancing conventional color prints, for adding color to monochrome prints and to enhance and add creative dashes of color to prints generated from a wide variety of media.

MARSHALL'S B&W PHOTO SETS

Marshall Black & White Photo sets feature professional black & white photographs by photographer, Cheryl Winser. Each set contains three pictures on a selected theme. The general directions and "before and after" pictures of each photograph appear on the back. These photographs are printed on semi-matte polycontrast paper. They can be hand colored with our oils, and they can be erased with a white vinyl eraser before they are fully dried.

"Still Life," "Pure Romance," and "Child Smiles," are 8" x 10" sets containing (3) black and white photographs each. "Kids at Play," "Fancy Flowers," and "Baby's Room" are 5 x 7 sets containing (3) black and white photographs each.

RETOUCH COLOR CHART

Group 1

| Primary Red | Primary Blue | Primary Yellow | Basic Black | Basic Blue | Basic Brown | Basic Flesh | Basic Green |

Group 2

| Basic Gray | Basic Violet | Bright Orange | Bright Red | Raw Sienna | Foliage Green | Verona Brown | Flesh Shadow |

Group 3

| Cheek | Burnt Sienna | Viridian | Aqua | Sky Blue | Oxide Green | Bright Violet | Lipstick Red |

SPOT ALL COLOR CHART

6BT

| Blue Black | Neutral Black | Selenium Brown | Sepia Tone | Brown Tone | Olive Tone |

3 B

| Blue Black | Neutral Black | Selenium Brown |

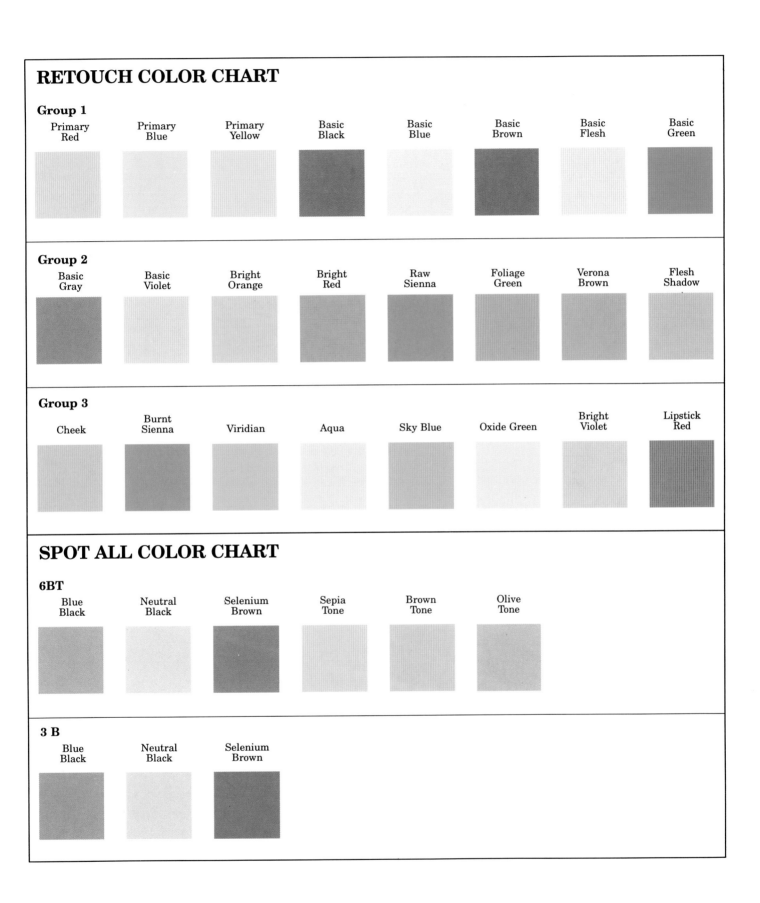

MARSHALL'S SABLE BRUSHES

You can apply Marshall's Oil colors with a wide variety of tools, including the cotton and skewers supplied with the kits, cotton balls, fine cloths, and so forth. However, for the finest control on details when applying oils, and for general use with Marshall's Retouch Colors and Spot-All Liquids, we recommend the lineup of Marshall's Red Sable Brushes. These brushes feature red sable bristles with seamless ferrules on laquered hardwood handles. For spotting, use the finer brushes, such as the #00000 (5/0) through #0; for larger area work, you can use any of the brushes up to the #2.

Brushes are identified by number codes, which indicated the relative size of the tip, or application end.

MARSHALL'S PROFESSIONAL SPRAYS

Print finishing is a way of protecting the efforts you have put into your work, plus makes for a more effective presentation when you show your work to friends, gallery owners or art directors. With this in mind, Marshall offers a full lineup of professional sprays. In addition, Marshall offers sprays for preparing the print surface for coloring, and helping the photographer tackle problems when doing still life photography.

HANDCOLORING PHOTOGRAPHS— THE VIDEO

By James A. McKinnis. Basic handcoloring technique. Mr. McKinnis handcolors a photograph from start to finish while explaining his techniques. You will learn all about the materials needed and will discover the best photographic enlarging papers so you can obtain optimum results handcoloring your own photographs. 50 minutes.

As with all sprays, work in a well-ventilated area, avoid direct contact and keep out of reach of children.

MARSHALL'S PROFESSIONAL SPRAYS

Product	Uses
Pre-Color	For those print surfaces which will not take Marshall's Oils, this spray helps provide some tooth for adherence.
Matte Finish	To provide a matte (non-glare) finish over any art medium.
Gloss Coat	Smudge- and moisture-proof, provides a clear, gloss finish.
Adhesive	Bonding for cardboard, foam rubber, plastic films, wood, cloth and metal. Water resistant.

MARSHALL'S COLORING AIDS

Coloring Aid	Use
P.M. Solution	As a pre-treatment for papers and a corrective solution for removing colors. When coloring with pencils, use P.M. Solution as a pre-treatment only if oils have not been applied.
Extender	A colorless neutral base which can be mixed with oils to reduce their saturation, or color strength. Use of more Extender yields paler colors. Can also be used for touchup or " clearing" color in small areas.
Marlene	For cleaning oils from print; best for touchups and minor corrections. (Use P.M. Solution to clear whole print, then finish with Marlene.) Use sparingly. Liquid needn't be wiped from print, as Marlene evaporates quickly.
Drier	Speeds up oil-color drying time from usual one to three days to about six hours. Invaluable when work area must be cleared for next project, or when working on deadlines.
Duolac	A quick-drying waterproof varnish. A smooth (satin) or glossy effect can be achieved by different brush-on methods, matter and effects.

ADDITIONAL MARSHALL'S PRODUCTS

Artist Wipes: Packaged in a convenient canister with a pop-up cover for easy dispensing of perforated wipes. They are tough enough to clean the messiest art tools yet gentle enough to wipe your hands because they contain a unique blend of natural citrus cleaners, plant extracts, jojoba oil, Vitamin E, aloe vera, wheat germ extract and biodegradable surfactania. No petroleum based solvents, perfumes or harsh chemicals are present. Clean-up is a snap and safe!

Blend-All Blender Pencil is colorless and allows you to blend colors smoothly with soft strokes. When handcoloring black & white photos with Marshall's Photo Oils and detailing with Marshall's Photo Pencils, you may use Marshall's Blend-All Colorless Blender Pencil to effortlessly blend the two mediums together.

Photo Mounts contains 250 - 1/2" self-adhesive mounts. Photo Corners contains 250 - 7/16" self-adhesive corners.

Oils may be purchased individually in 1/2 x 2" tubes. Pencils may also be purchased separately.

OTHER MATERIALS FOR HANDCOLORING

While the lineup of Marshall's products provides virtually all the art materials you'll need for your work, here are some other items recommended to make the work easier. Many of these items are available through your specialty photo or art supply dealer. Check the Brandess/Kalt/Aetna Photographic & Video Accessories Buying Guide, available through your photo dealer who stocks Marshall products, for information on many of these materials.

Working Surfaces: The importance of a perfectly flat, non-textured working surface cannot be overemphasized. Any surface with texture or stipple may actually transfer that pattern onto the print, especially when you're hand-rubbing oils. And, if you're working with thin, single-weight papers, any roughness on the working surface may abrade the print during your work.

The rule is—if you run your fingernail over the surface and hear a rippling sound or feel any texture, do not use it as a working surface. Old tabletops, desktops or drafting tables with splotched paint or other materials imbedded in the surface can cause problems, as any surface imperfection may well show up in the print.

Drafting Tape: As you work a print, you may find that the momentum of your hand causes it to move. Though you can hold it down with your free hand, it's usually best to tack it down to your working surfae. This is best accomplished with drafting tape, or any tape that will not abrade the print surface when you lift it away. You needn't cover large areas of the print with the tape- just the edges or the corners.

Cotton Balls, Cotton Swabs: While most of the Photo Oil kits contain skewers and cotton tufts, you'll eventually have to replenish your supply. Available in most drug stores or pharmacies, fine-quality 100% pure cotton can be wadded to pick up oil colors from your palette or wrapped on skewers for fine-area control. Cotton swabs also come in handy for certain areas. When purchasing cotton, be sure to get the finest grade available, as inexpensive materials may leave wisps or hairs behind when you work. The use of 100% pure long-fiber cotton is key, as cotton with other filaments or fibers could cause colors to spread or disappear too rapidly.

Cotton Gloves: It is important that you protect the surface on which you're applying color from fingerprints and handprints that may leave an oily residue. Many retouchers and handcolorists wear cotton gloves while working.

Palette, Palette Dishes: While some handcolorists work directly from the tube, most choose to spread a small amount of oil onto a palette and blend and mix colors as they work. This is probably the best method for mixing colors or for adding Extender to lessen the strength of colors. You can use glass, plexiglass or any hard, non-absorbent surface as a palette.

When using Photo Retouch Colors or Spot-All Liquids, use a dish-type palette, such as those used by watercolorists. These come in handy whether you work "wet" or "dry", two techniques we'll cover later.

Pressurized Dusters and Static Eliminator Brushes: While a clean working area is important, you can not always control dust, loose fibers or even some flaking that may appear on the surface of the print. A burst from a can of pressurized air will clear these problems, thus avoid corrective procedures later. You can also use a blower brush or a static-eliminator brush for this purpose.

Erasers: High-quality plastic erasers come in handy when doing fine pencil work, clearing highlights or even for buffing oils. As this book went to press, Marshall's has plans to add such an eraser to its product lineup.

Drying Area: Whether you work with oils or apply a protective spray coat after completion you should have an area ready in which you can store the print. This may be a drying rack, shelf or other surface that is free from dust, pets and the curious hands of children.

Light Source: While you can work in normal room light, having a fairly bright light source illuminate the print while you work is recommended. This will quickly show off any flaws, overlaps of color or other small details that may not be obvious under lower levels of light. In addition, this will clearly show the differences in subtle colors that you apply. A small table-mounted lamp with a high-intensity bulb is good, although any gooseneck style lamp that won't interfere with your work will do.

Remember, although the human optical system adjusts for different color temperatures of light, colors will still look slightly different under different light sources, so choose your light source with this in mind. For critical work, you may want to work under a daylight-balanced light-source or other high-quality lamp.

Magnifying Glass or Loupe: For critical work, the use of a magnifying glass or loupe can come in handy. Many retouchers and colorists use a magnifying glass attached to a gooseneck-type holder for close inspection of details.

Work Prints: Although you can work directly on what will be your final print, it's useful to have a "work print"—one that was printed at the same time on the same type of paper—as a testing guide. Each type of paper will have a slightly different response to colors. For example, a warm-tone, chlorobromide paper has a creamy-white base, while a cold-tone paper has a brighter, more neutral white base. Each of these base whites act as an undercoating, and can effect the final look of the colors you apply. Have a work print handy and use it to test each color as you procede.

As you work with these materials, you may find other tools that are particularly suited to your needs. Don't be afraid to improvise, or to use various applicators in your work. For example, some handcolorists use a frisket to cover a certain area when they work, which they remove later to add another color. Others work carefully and remove color from select areas with Marlene or a fine-point plastic eraser. We'll explore these methods, and more, as we move on to the techniques of working with Marshall materials, and as we discover how each artist uses various materials in their work.

Working with the Materials

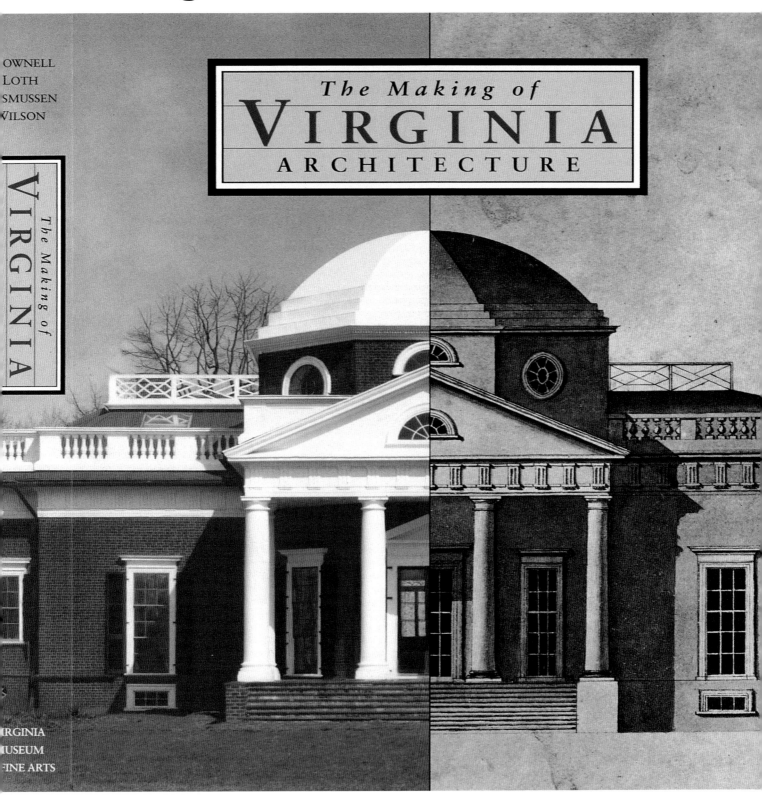

OWNELL
LOTH
SMUSSEN
VILSON

The Making of
VIRGINIA

The Making of
VIRGINIA
ARCHITECTURE

IRGINIA
IUSEUM
INE ARTS

Photo Oils and Pencils

PREPARING THE SURFACE

Before you begin to think about what colors you'll be applying to your image, consider the surface of the print itself. By far the most receptive surface for handcoloring with oils and pencils is a flat, matte one. For photographers, this means choosing a fiber-based or resin-coated matte printing paper. The RC papers offer processing convenience, as they dry quickly and without curl.

For those working on non-photographic prints, such as thermal prints, images from color copiers and other computer-generated imagery, test the colors on a work print. While the Marshall's materials are specially formulated for photographs they can also be used on a wide variety of other imaging media.

The reason matte papers are favored is that they simply have a better "tooth" or holding surface for oils and pencils than do glossy or satin-type finishes. If you have no choice and are coloring on a glossy or satin finish, there are two ways to help gain "tooth" for color application.

One is to use Marshall's Pre-Color Spray over the surface. While this does provide a grip surface for the colors, it becomes the actual skin on which the colors are applied. This surface, while usually better than a non-sprayed one, may in fact resist color changes and even lift off if too much force is applied when colors are laid down. In some cases, Marshall's P.M. Solution can also be used on non-matte surfaces to help create a better environment for the color.

If you are using pencils for coloring, use of the P.M. Solution on any surface—matte or otherwise—is recommended to help with color blending. However, this is not necessary if you are using pencils in combination with oils, as the oils provide the medium for the pencil colors. You can use pencils without any surface preparation on a matte print, but each "stroke" of the pencil will show.

Some artists do work on glossy papers, and their use is certainly not precluded. However, all in all, if given a choice, work with a matte or semi-matte print surface.

PRINT COLOR, PRINT DENSITY

Consideration should also be given to the type of paper and the printing technique for images that are to be handcolored. This involves the "image color" of the paper and the degree of density—or tonal richness—of the print. As the colors are transparent, whatever color sits underneath will effect the final hue. In black-and-white papers, the image color can range from what's known as "cold" to "warm", with cold papers having bright, white highlights and deep, almost bluish blacks, and warm papers having creamy white highlights and near-brownish blacks. Many papers are neutral, or sit somewhere between these two extremes, or can be pushed in one direction or another through the use of different developers.

Print density has a profound effect on how applied color "reads." Here, image above was printed 1 stop lighter; same colors were applied to both. (Photo, coloring, © George Schaub.)

PHOTOGRAPHIC PAPERS FOR HANDCOLORING

While handcolorists work on virtually every brand and surface of paper, the following are those which have surfaces that are most conductive to the application of photo oils and pencils. Matte is preferable; semi-matte is the next best thing. Brand names and surfaces change over time. Check with your photo dealer for any up-to-date list. The listing here shows the manufacturer, paper brand name, the surface and whether the paper is fiber-based or resin-coated.

Manufacturer	Paper	Surface/Code	Fiber	RC
Agfa	Brovira-Speed	Semi-Matte / 312 PE		✔
Agfa	Multicontrast Premium RC	Semi-Matte / MC 312		✔
Agfa	Multicontrast Classic	Semi-Matte / 118	✔	
Agfa	Portriga-Speed	Semi-Matte / 318 PE		✔
Arista	Classic Fiber Base	Matte	✔	
Arista	Variable Contrast Fiber Base	Matte	✔	
Cachet	Multibrome WA-VCFB Plus	Full Matte	✔	
Cachet	Multi-Speed WA-VCRC	Matte		✔
Cachet	Structura Lux - flax cloth	Matte	✔	
Forte	Elegance Bromofort	Matte	✔	
Forte	Salon RC	Semi-Matte		✔
Ilford	Ilfobrom Galerie FB	Matte / 5K	✔	
Ilford	Multigrade FB Warmtone	Semi-Matte / 24K	✔	
Ilford	Multigrade IV RC	Pearl / 44M		✔
Ilford	Multigrade RC Warmtone	Pearl / 44M		✔
Ilford	Multigrade IV RC Portfolio	Pearl / 44K		✔
Ilford	Multigrade FB	Matte / 5K	✔	
Ilford	Multigrade IV RC	Satin / 25M		✔
Kodak	Kodabrome II RC	Semi-Matte / N		✔
Kodak	Polycontrast III RC	Semi-Matte / N		✔
Kodak	Polyfiber	Semi-Matte / N	✔	
Kodak	Polymax RC	Semi-Matte / N		✔
Kodak	Polymax Fine-Art	Semi-Matte / N	✔	
Kodak	P-Max Art RC	High Matte		✔
Luminos	Flexicon VCS	Semi-Matte		✔
Luminos	RCR Art	Matte		✔
Luminos	Charcoal R	Rough	✔	
Luminos	Tapestry X	Texture	✔	

A ✔ indicates availability

In general, handcolorists choose to work on warm tone papers, or tone their papers in either sepia, brown or other sulphide-type toning baths to give them a "warm" undercoat. This is especially true for those working on portraits, and generally true for people working with nature scenes and still lifes. Not everyone follows this, but those that do say that it is much more conducive to the hand coloring medium.

The density or tonal values of the print also have a profound effect on the way colors look when applied. While the oils come in different strengths, the print density upon which they are applied—be it open shadows, bright highlights or dark areas with detail—will have a marked effect on how that color reads. Thus, if you want color to dominate the scene and define the image, work on a lighter print; if you want less color emphasis use a darker version of the same print. To see the effect of print density on results, make a series of prints of the same scene, each one successively darker than the other, and add any color you desire. The results will be quite revealing.

In general, many handcolorists tend to favor lighter prints, and even dodge areas where there is too much shadow density. If you don't do your own printing, work with a lab that will follow your printing instructions. Some handcolorists prepare or order prints with paper-white highlights, knowing they can either add color later, or use that highlight for a graphic counterpoint in the overall work. You can also bleach (reduce) print density yourself with the potassium ferricyanide/hypo (Kodak's Farmers Reducer) method. In addition, most toning baths will bleach prints back (reduce density).

While to most people handcoloring of an image may be an afterthought, experienced handcolorists actually photograph with handcoloring in mind. For some, that may mean working with high-grain films (such as black-and-white infrared film); for others it could mean using filters to emphasize clouds in skys or to add extra contrast to a closeup of a leaf. Of course, the image itself is key, but intentionally using the tricks of the photographic craft to add to the overall graphic appeal will enhance your results.

WARM-TONED PHOTOGRAPHIC PAPERS

The following papers have a decidedly warm image color, and are available with surfaces that are conducive to applying color. Brand names and availability change, so check with your photo dealer. Other papers can be toned in sulphide-type toners to give them a "warmer" color.

Manufacturer	Paper Name	Comments
Agfa	Portriga-Rapid	Creamy-whites, available in Grades 1-3.
Agfa	Portriga-Speed	The RC version of Portriga-Rapid.
Cachet	Expo-WA	Neutral black warm tone in Grades 2 & 3.
Forte	Fortezo Elegance	Available in Exhibition (heavy) weight.
Ilford	Multigrade RC Warmtone	Rich, warm blacks, creamy whites
Ilford	Multigrade FB Warmtone	Warm image color, creamy white base, velvety blacks
Kodak	Ektalure G	Available in "normal" (approx. #2) only.
Kodak	Polyfiber G	Cold tone, but with creamy whites.

To emphasize the warmth in these papers, develop in a warm-tone developer, such as Kodak Selectol, Kodak Selectol Soft, Agfa Neutol WA, Ethol LPD (warm-working dilution) or Edwal Platinum II developer. You can also enhance the warmth of any paper by toning in a sulphide-type toner.

APPLICATION AND BLENDING

The general method for applying color is to lay it on the print then to rub it down. If you're working with oils, squeeze a small amount from the tube onto a hard, non-absorbent surface, then pick it up with cotton wrapped around a skewer, or a cotton ball. Place the color onto the print in as broad or small an area as needed, then rub that color in with a clean piece of cotton.

When putting colors on the print, cover broader areas, such as sky or grass, entirely with one color before going to the next. Don't be too concerned about color that goes in the wrong area, as that's easy to correct later. In addition, you can cover the first color with the second, or rub down the first color so much that it literally disappears from the print. In short, apply the color to the print then use a smooth and gentle circular motion to rub it in with cotton.

If you're only working with pencils, lightly apply the color over the prepared surface of the print, then blend and rub in colors with the cotton, just as you do with the oils. You can leave the "stroke" of the pencil intact, or work in colors by rubbing. Some handcolorists use nylon fabric or hosiery to burnish in pencils or oils for a soft effect.

© Grace Schaub 1994

For this deep forest scene the mood was set using a variety of Marshall's Oils and Pencils. For the rocks, several oil colors were applied sparingly one over another with long fiber cotton, then rubbed gently into the surface of the print. A plastic eraser was used to clean the edges of any unwanted color and also to clear highlights on the rocks in the foreground. For the ferns, tree bark and foliage an assortment of Marshall's Pencils were used, with lighter and darker variations of color applied to emphasize highlight and shadow details.

Portrait Painting with Photo Oils: Master photographer and artist Linda Weaver suggests these step-by-step techniques for portraits. (More of Weaver's work appears later in this guide.) "Photographs to be oil painted should be printed on fiber-based paper...It is best to tone the prints...Before being painted, photographs should be mounted to keep them flat. A guide print is very helpful in retaining a likeness.

(# 1) Highlights: With cotton on the end of a wooden skewer, rub a light coat of Raw Sienna on the main highlight area of the face.

(# 2) Middletones: Mix Marshall's Flesh and Basic Flesh about half and half. Add enough Marshall's White to achieve the same tonal value as the middletones in the face. Apply this mixture with cotton, overlapping the highlight color. With cotton, lightly rub out the highlights.

(# 3) Shadows: In the darkest shadows, lightly rub in Combination Flesh Shadow to give more depth. Blend with the middletones.

(# 4) Cheeks and Lips: Gently apply a warm red, such as Vermilion or Cheek, blending it with the flesh color. If the teeth show, clean them off with Marlene. Lightly paint them off-white, keeping the same tonal value as shown on the photograph.

(# 5) Eyes: Paint the eyes with a small pointed brush. With cotton on the end of a tiny wooden skewer, blend the iris color. Place the catchlight at one or eleven o'clock, depending on the direction of light. Paint the crease over the eyelid with the Combination Flesh Shadow. Rub Marshall's White in the white part of the eye, graying it as it gets closer to the top eyelid.

Paint the upper lashes with one of the browns, such as Verona or Sepia, using the small pointed brush. Lightly brush in the eyebrows (same color as the hair) and blend with cotton to look soft.

(# 6) Hair and Background: Apply the hair color with cotton on the end of the wooden skewer. Rub out the highlights to retain the shape of the hair. A mixture of Marshall's Grayed Background Green mixed with Verona brown and White is great for transparent oil backgrounds. Apply this with cotton, blending it with the hair color to look soft. Dacron instead of cotton may be used for blending. Rub in the clothing color with cotton and blend with Dacron. Rub out the highlights and lightly brush in shadow color. This completes a transparent oil.

(# 7) Brush Oil Technique: Follow steps one through six, omitting the background. Paint the background with larger brushes, applying the paint with a bristle brush and blending with a sable. Lightly brush in more hair color, blending it with a background color while both are still wet. Brush in highlight color in the hair. (For example, for blonde hair, Raw Sienna and White with Verona Brown in the shadows; for auburn hair, Verona Brown with Burnt Sienna in the highlights; for gray hair, Sepia with White.) Brush in more color on the clothing, building up the highlights.

(# 8) "Velvet Flesh": You may continue to build up the flesh color by applying the paint thicker with a sable brush. It is very important that the flesh mixture be the same tonal value as the print. Additional flesh colors may be mixed for this, such as vermillion, yellow and white. An oil portrait looks better varnished. After it is completely dry to the touch you may spray retouch varnish on it for a rich, luster finish. If the customer insists on putting the painting under glass, do not varnish."

Mixing colors is part of the fun of working with these materials. The rules of color apply—yellow plus blue equals green, red plus yellow equals orange, and so forth. Because the method of oil application is to place color on the print and then rub it in, mixing should take place off the print surface, on a palette. Squeeze a small amount of each color on the palette, then mix the colors together using a palette knife or similar tool.

Once the color is mixed, the only way to see how it looks is to place it on the print and blend it in. The color on the palette will appear too opaque to make a final color call.

While there are a wide variety of colors in the Marshall's line that can be used "straight" or mixed, there are certain techniques that yield an even wider range of colors for your palette. You can, for example, change the character of a color itself, without creating a new color. Or, you can create more subdued colors and vary their strength as desired.

For example, to make a color less brilliant without changing its essential hue, simply mix a small portion of its complement into it before you put in on the print. Thus, if the yellow from the tube is too bright for your needs, add a touch of violet; if the red's not quite right, a taste of green will subdue it. Adding too much will change the nature of the color itself, or turn it gray—experimentation is key. If you're unsure about color complements, invest in a "color wheel", a visual aid available in art supply stores.

If the color is too strong, add a dab of Extender, mix it in, and then apply it to the print and rub it in. Start with 1/2 as much Extender in volume as color, then go 1:1, 2:1 and so forth. Experimentation, and the needs of each image, is key here.

The way in which you mix and match color on the print also effects the perception of each color. Keep in mind that while the density of the print will effect color, working with different colors in the shadow, mid-tone and highlight areas of even the same subject may enhance the effect further. There are scores of ideas and color techniques that can be used, many of which are displayed in the Gallery section.

CLEARING HIGHLIGHTS/ CORRECTING COLORS

The beauty of working with Marshall's Oils and Pencils is the ease with which they can be changed and manipulated, right on the print. To lighten a color once it is applied, simply rub it down—the harder you rub the lighter the color. If you want to lift color off the print entirely, use cotton lightly moistened with Marlene or P.M. Solution (the former for smaller areas of color, the latter for clearing large sections or a whole print.) And, if color gets into an area in which you want another color, simply add the new color over the old.

The same ease applies to adding color to or subtracting color from small details, such as white picket fences in front of green lawns, or sailboats on vast seas. Color the larger areas first, without being concerned about getting color in your details. Simply lift the color from the small area with Marlene applied with a fine brush, or with the fine point of a Marshall's Pencil. Highlights can be handled in the same way. You can also add color to small details and highlights with Marshall's Pencils, which are specifically made to blend with the Oils.

DRY DOWN

Once you have finished your work on a print, allow it to dry in a dust-free area for at least two or three days before touching the surface. Depending upon conditions, the final dry-down before you spray or varnish the print should be at least a week. To speed drying, you can use Marshall's Drier, which will allow you to handle the print within about six hours, and to varnish or overcoat it within a day. And to preserve the print, especially when the original may go to art directors or through prepress operations, consider working with Marshall's Duolac varnish.

The varnish provides a waterproof coating in either a glossy or dull finish. For a dull finish pour some Duolac on the print and spread it with a lintless cloth. After a few minutes, remove the excess Duolac with a clean, dry cloth. For a glossy finish, apply Duolac with a brush, first brushing vertically, then horizontally. The more the Duolac left on the print the higher the gloss effect.

Self-expression is the name of the game. Approach, application of materials and color all play a creative part in evoking a particular mood. Here, two interpretations of the same scene, each with its own distinct mood and sense of place, are created by choosing different color schemes and depth. Having several prints of an image gives you the opportunity to explore the materials in different ways, and to create very different interpretations of the same scene.

31

TOP TEN TIPS ON USING
MARSHALL'S OILS AND PENCILS

The way you use color will be dictated by the image and your personal taste, and the only way you will discover that is to work with the materials. As you do so, keep these pointers in mind:

1 Keep tubes capped when not in use. If the caps are left off and the color hardens, pierce the hardened color with a skewer or other thin wire. If color hardens inside the tube, adding Extender can give it new life.

2 Do not take color directly from the tube, as this may be wasteful (you'll quickly learn how little color it takes to cover a fairly large area in a print) and you may get color "skins" or separated oil. The best technique is to squeeze a small amount onto a palette or hard surface, then mix and pick up for application as required.

3 Keep your applicator clean, as colors may inadvertantly blend, and don't be afraid to go through lots of cotton balls, swabs and skewered tufts. Change cotton frequently when working. Long-fiber, 100% cotton is best.

4 Test colors on new media, and have a work print handy. While colors are easy to remove, testing color effects on prints similar to the original will help you work cleanly and efficiently.

5 When clearing or cleaning colors with Marlene some hard edges may form around the area that's been cleaned. Blend these, and any other hard color edges in your print, with dry cotton.

6 Be sure that the surface area on which you're working is clean, flat and free from any obstructions. This will prevent any tearing or bending of a print during rubdown.

7 Allied with the above, don't be hesitatant to rub the print with as much force as necessary to get the color and effect you desire. Excessive force is unneccesary; however, with too light a touch, you may not achieve your desired effect.

8 As you work, start to make a catalog of colors on a variety of papers. Get to know the materials and how they work on different brands of paper, different surfaces and even on those same papers processed in various developers. While some of the effects are subtle, others can truly change the character of your work.

9 Don't hesitate to use Pencils and Oils together. The Pencils have their own character, but when used with Oils they make highlighting and color detailing easy.

10 Experiment! The whole Marshall System has been designed to make application, blending and correction simple.

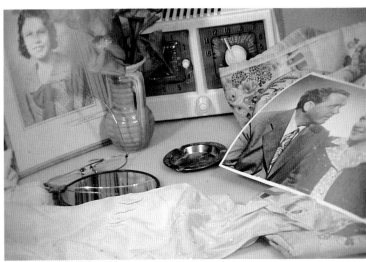

Transforming monochrome prints to full-color scenes allows for a very personal rendition that expresses whatever mood the artist desires. The wide variety of colors and coloring aids can be used to obtain virtually every color and color intensity, from deep, rich shades to soft pastels.

Though originally photographed on color negative film, this image was later printed in black and white on Agfa Portriga Rapid paper and handcolored. According to the artist, Curtice Taylor, this allowed for a greater control of color and creation of mood in the scene, and gave him the ability to enhance tones and color combinations. This image was used as part of a photo essay on the Paris Flea Markets.

Marshall's Photo Retouch Colors

Marshall's Photo Retouch Colors come in a wide variety of colors which can be blended or used "straight", depending upon your needs. Most are concentrated colors, thus require some dilution to match the color on your print; however, some commonly-used colors are made to be used directly from the bottle. These colors can be used on a wide variety of media, including black-and-white prints, Polaroid color prints, conventional color paper and color copies and other computer-generated print media.

The variations of color you can obtain are virtually endless. You can mix colors, add water to weaken color or use various color combinations straight from the bottle. You can also remove or lighten color after it has been applied, though it's best to work lighter than required and build up color as you go. To get a sense of the wide varieties of color and tones you can achieve, take out a work print on any media, and mix various colors in a watercolor palette or small glass or porcelain dish. Start with color straight from the bottle and brush it on to the print. Then add a drop or two of water and apply as before.

You'll begin to build a catalog of colors, and see the effects of both dilution and mixing with other colors. Eventually you'll get a feel for the colors and how they respond, and how dilution effects strength. This flexibility will quickly translate to greater control and creativity in your work.

The main difference between working with Marshall's Photo Retouch Colors and Marshall's Photo Oils and Pencils is that the Retouch Colors penetrate the emulsion of the print while the other media sit on top of the emulsion. This means that you can easily work on glossy-type surfaces with the Retouch Colors. You may also find that you use all three (oils, pencils, retouch colors) on one print.

APPLYING THE COLORS

To apply the colors you'll need watercolor brushes. These brushes, manufactured by Marshall, come in various point sizes. You should also have a fine-pore cellulose sponge and lintless blotter paper to help take up color. A watercolor palette, or small glasses are good for holding and mixing colors.

You should also have some clear water and facial tissue for cleansing the brush of color between applications. Use blotting or similar paper to cover any portion of the print on which you lean the heel of your hand as you work. Be sure to work under good lighting, as this will help you see the exact colors that are going on the print and aid when working finely detailed portions of the image. Finally, make sure that the working surface on which you place the print is smooth; holding the print down firmly with drafting tape is also a good idea.

As these colors soak into the emulsion, it is always a good idea to work lighter and build up color with successive applications. These colors can be removed, but following the lighter to darker rule will save you corrective steps later.

Use a workprint (the same medium on which the image to be worked on is printed) to test your colors. Apply the color with a brush, either with a stippling motion or a stroke, and compare the

RETOUCH COLOR KITS

Retouch Colors are available in kits, with each kit containing 8 assorted colors in dropper-type bottles.

Set #	Primary Colors	Basic Colors	Bright Colors
RC-1	Yellow, Red, Blue	Flesh, Green, Brown, Black, Blue	
RC-2		Gray, Raw Sienna, Flesh Shadow Verona Brown, Violet, Foliage Green	Red, Orange
RC-3		Lipstick Red, Sky Blue, Oxide Green, Aqua, Viridian, Cheek, Burnt Sienna	Violet

strength of the color with that which is needed on your original print. If the color seems too strong, dilute with water. Make your corrections in small steps, and, when you first work with the colors, don't expect to get it right on your early attempts.

The media on which you work, and the type of work you're doing, will determine how you work with these colors. For example, if you're color "spotting", that is, correcting dust or lint marks that resulted from lack of cleanliness in the darkroom, you work with complementary colors. This applies only to the following color spots, or defects: green, orange, red, violet and yellow. Use Primary Blue for the orange spots and bring the strength up to match the surrounding area; use Primary Red on green spots; use Primary Yellow on violet spots. Apply Violet (a mix of Primary Red and Blue) to yellow spots; and Green (a mixture of Primary Blue and Yellow) to red spots.

To match colors of surrounding areas on most color images, merely mix from various bottles until you obtain the color you desire. Then, build up that color on the print to the desired strength.

Some retouchers like to work on a wet surface, as they feel this blends the colors more easily. This is especially effective when working large areas. However, be sure that the media on which you're working will not be adversely effected by this procedure, and that dry-down will not result in emulsion shrinkage that might cause cracks or bubbles. The wet method works fine with black-and-white and most conventional color papers, but be sure to test with a workprint before trying it on any original. Keep in mind that when wet most conventional color papers will have a color cast, ranging from blue to magenta. That means that you should allow the prints to dry before making final color judgements. You can speed the process with a hair dryer, but be sure to keep the temperature low and the hair dryer a safe distance from the print so that you don't damage the delicate emulsion.

REMOVING RETOUCH COLORS

The best technique is to work slowly and carefully and build color as you go. However, there will be times when you over-color or change your mind once a color has been applied. In those instances, you can lighten the color, or remove it entirely. The best method is to prepare a bottle of "color remover" which you can use whenever necessary. It's a simple matter: add 1 drop of liquid household bleach to 10 drops of water.

To lighten color, apply the mix over the Retouch Color and let it stand until the approximate shade has been attained; you stop the bleaching action by first blotting off the color remover then covering the area with water. Then, add water again and let it spread a bit to make sure the bleach has been thoroughly removed. Blot again, and you're ready to reapply color or let the print stay as it is. Experiment with this technique on workprints, and you'll soon get the knack.

This color removal technique can also be used to clear highlights, open up details within larger color blocks for different colors, and to touch up any over-coloring that may have occured.

Liquid Retouch Colors can be used for both corrective and creative work on conventional color prints (plus many other media as well .) Here, the original image of white blossoms is intensified and transformed with Retouch Colors. All colors, which were diluted slightly prior to application, were applied to the print with a #2 Brush.

USING RETOUCH COLORS AS A TONER

While the Retouch Colors are usually used for touch-up and selective coloring, you can color the entire print by immersing it in a single or mixed color/water bath. You can also dip part of the print in—such as a sky or ground horizon—then remove some of the colors by the technique described above. You can also cover parts of the print with a resist, such as a liquid frisket, and either leave it uncolored or add other colors later. After the bath, remove the frisket.

USING RETOUCH COLORS ON TRANSPARENCY FILM

Marshall's Retouch Colors can be used to add color and impact to title slides, or to do corrective retouching on any slide. Once you have prepared a title on a copy board and photographed it with high-contrast film, simply immerse the processed film in "straight" or diluted Retouch Color, or brush the color on the emulsion side of the slide in select areas.

SUBDUING RETOUCH COLORS

Like most Marshall's materials, the Retouch Colors can be mixed to obtain an infinite variety of tones and shades. If you want to subdue the Retouch Colors (if they are too bright or strong for your needs) follow the chart below. Note: to lighten colors, just add water.

If retouch color is too:	Add:
Red	Green
Yellow	Violet
Blue	Orange
Green	Red
Orange	Blue
Brown	Blue plus a little Yellow
Yellow-Green	Blue plus Violet
Reddish-Blue	Yellow plus Green
Bluish-Green	Orange plus Red
Bright Red	Blue plus Green

For retouching pictorial slides you also work on the emulsion (dull) side of the image. However, some slides have a coating, or lacquer, over both sides. If this is the case, you should clear the emulsion side with Marlene by using a cotton tuft and rubbing it gently, but firmly, over the slide surface.

Though you can work with a mounted slide, it's usually a good idea to remove it from the mount and fasten it with a non-abrasive tape onto a lightbox. First test the color by applying it to a slide similar to the one which you are about to color. Once the color tests, use a #1or #3 brush for large areas; for smaller areas, use a #000 through #0 brush. For small areas, you may have to use a magnifying glass for inspection; magnifiers attached to gooseneck stands, which brace onto tables or are free standing, are best for this work.

When you apply color, work as "dry" as possible. If excess liquid is applied, quickly remove it with a sponge or lintless blotter paper. If you're coloring large areas, such as sky, it's a good idea to first moisten that area with water—this makes the surface more receptive to color. If the applied color is too dark, apply clear water to the area and let it stand for about a minute, then blot it. If you want to clear or lighten the entire slide, immerse it in water before the color "sets."

As with all materials described in this guide, start light, then build colors as you work. However, if you intend to project slides, be aware that a somewhat stronger color is best, as the intensity of the light will tend to diminish the color's intensity.

OTHER MEDIA

Retouch Colors can be used on virtually any media, provided that the colors will absorb into the surface. They can be used on thermal paper, laser copy paper, Polaroid prints, gum bichromate images on watercolor paper, and so forth.

However, it is strongly recommended that you test how the colors take, and how their water-based quality effects the media on which you work. Always test on a workprint first; test how the color takes, how the liquid may diffuse throughout the paper, and how the colors match those that may be particular to the media. As you know, the dyes used in certain media are quite different than those used in conventional silver-based images. The diversity of the Retouch Colors allows for great freedom in color mixing and matching.

Spot-All Liquids

The Marshall's Spot-All Liquids are specially formulated for retouching on every type of black-and-white paper, as well as toned black-and-white prints, and black-and-white negatives. The dyes can be applied with brushes, cotton swabs or airbrush equipment.

The dyes come in a variety of "colors", or tones which can be mixed and matched for every spotting problem. Black-and-white papers vary in their "tone", or image color, depending upon the brand and type of paper, the developer in which they are processed, and the toner, if any, in which they are bathed after processing. Each of these variables causes a shift in image color.

For example, a warm-tone black and white paper developed in a cold-tone developer will have a decidedly different cast than when developed in a warm-tone developer. And, a cold-tone paper will have a different image color than a warm-tone paper when both are toned in sepia toner. The range of image colors, and the subtleties that differentiate them, is quite wide. To meet this challenge, the entire gamut of color possibilities can be obtained when working either "straight" or with blended colors using the Spot-All Liquid dyes.

GETTING READY

For most purposes, fine-tipped brushes are best for spotting and retouching. Have a selection available, starting with a #000 and up through a #0 (the more zeroes, the finer the point.) You will also need a sponge and lintless blotters, plus a watercolor-type palette for mixing colors. While some dyes can be used right from the bottle, you'll find that blending various dyes will yield just the colors you require. You can pre-blend the colors in a palette dish, allow them to dry, then use a moistened tip of the brush to add a touch of water immediately before application.

For example, if you have a warm/neutral image color on the print, you might use a dye made from combining one drop of Olive Tone with two drops of Neutral Black; or, for a moderately cold-tone print you may need a mix made from one drop of Blue Black with two of Neutral Black.

When you combine these dyes in your palette, mark the mix and how it was made with indelible marker on the lip of the palette well. This saves time later. In addition, as you work with the dyes, you'll find that you use some dyes and dye combinations more consistently than others, especially if your paper choice and processing procedures are also consistent.

PRINT SPOTTING

Unless you or your printmaker work in a dust-free environment, you're going to have some trouble with spots on your black-and-white prints. These spots are formed by dust and lint, either on the negative itself or on some part of the light path in the enlarger. These flecks, large or small, show up as white blemishes and, if not removed, will detract from the look of the image. Remember, when you enlarge a negative you also enlarge any dust that may reside upon it, so even a small imperfection can become obvious.

Try to avoid these blemishes, as spotting is not a "fun" part of print finishing. Indeed, it can be tedious and, at times, frustrating. When you print, clean your negatives with a burst of condensed air, or wipe them with a camel hair or anti-static cloth. If there is dirt imbedded in the negative—usually as a result of drying in a dusty area—you probably have to rewash the negative to remove it. Also, check your enlarger for dust particles, and keep your enlarging lens clean. And, if you get dust-laden prints, or even blemished prints back from your lab, send them back and insist upon cleaner work.

TESTING COLORS

However, even with the greatest care, there will be times when some spotting is unavoidable. When you begin to spot, use a sheet of the same photographic paper as the original (such as a test print that was printed and developed at the same time the original was made), and test your colors on the workprint. If you're working directly from the bottle, or if you're working from freshly-mixed dye, you must purge the liquid from the brush and work with as dry a tip as possible. Too wet a tip will result in too much dye being spread on the print surface, which makes what must be a tightly controlled process difficult to control. If you're working from dry mix that sits on your palette, touch the tip of the brush on a moist sponge, and then pick up color.

Make a few strokes on the workprint to be sure the color matches. Remember, a mismatched image color is probably as distracting to print quality as is the spot itself. If the color matches you can procede—if not, try different combinations.

When you begin, pick dye up from the palette in the manner described above and start with those spots that are in the denser (darkest) area of the image. First, make a few strokes of the brush on the test print until you see that the dye laid down is slightly lighter than the darkest tone in the area of the print which you're spotting.

Rather than work in broad strokes, and try to cover the blemish in one shot, you must work in a stippling fashion. Using the tip of the brush, work as if you're dotting the i's and spot from the center of the blemish out to the edges. Work slowly and carefully, and be sure to build density as you go.

For example, if you have to spot a straight line or a hairline, consider that line a series of dots. Work with the grain of the image if you can. Keep the brush nearly vertical and use only the tip—don't jab the area so that more dye spreads than you need. Use a light touch, and dab the spot away.

As you work you'll notice that the color coming off the brush becomes lighter—this is an excellent time to work on spots in the less-dense areas of the print, if needed. The key is to work dark to light, and to keep the brush slightly moist rather than wet. Be patient—spotting can be a difficult task to master. However, as the cliche goes, practice does make perfect, and you'll soon get the "touch" that makes for a good spotter.

CLEARING DYE

Of course, even the most professional spotters make mistakes—they apply too much dye or too dark a dye, or even the wrong color dye onto the print. Fortunately, these mistakes can be voided. Mix a solution of household bleach in a 1:10 ratio (1 part bleach to 10 parts water.) Take a tuft of cotton wrapped on a skewer and wet it, then take a similar applicator and place the bleach solution on the spot. When it has faded to where you want it, remove the bleach with the wet cotton. Avoid using a good brush for the bleaching procedure, as it will eventually ruin it. Also, do not overdo this corrective procedure, as the bleach can be difficult to control and may in fact discolor the print. Practice this technique on work prints before trying it on masters.

The most important thing to remember about spotting is that you are building density, and not trying to match the surrounding tone and density in one stroke. In some cases, keeping the spotted area slightly lighter than the surround is both acceptable and a way to ensure that you're doing it right. And, if you find that you have to spot all your prints, take steps to correct the problem in your enlarger or your darkroom. If you spend too much time spotting you'll come to appreciate the benefits of printing clean.

SPOT-ALL LIQUIDS: COLORS AND THEIR USES

Blue Black	For cold-tone papers
Selenium Brown	For warm, reddish-brown tones, for selenium-toned prints
Neutral Black	For neutral-toned papers, most variable contrast papers
Sepia Tone	Yellowish-brown for warm- and neutral tone sepia-toned prints
Brown Tone	For brown-toned and polytoners that impart a brown color
Olive Tone	For warm-toned papers when developed in cold-tone developer
These colors can be mixed to match virtually any image color.	

Handcoloring and New Image Making Tools and Media

Photographers, illustrators and artists today are being introduced to a new generation of imaging equipment, including digital cameras, image manipulation software and various hard-copy output devices (printers) dedicated to these imaging systems. While this type of imaging is in its infancy, there already exists a large number of artists working in the medium, among them "converts" from conventional illustration and photography.

While the hardware of these new imaging modalities are quite different from those of the past, the media on which hard copy prints are made does not differ much from either conventional photographic or copy paper. In fact, manufacturers have done their best to match the characteristics of familiar photographic papers, finding that public acceptance is usually wider when they do so. And, even though output by a computer, these prints are not infallible, and will often need spotting, color correction or enhancement by hand.

All Marshall's materials, including oils, pencils, retouch colors and spotting liquids, can be used in the same fashion with these imaging materials as with conventional papers. The same procedures apply for adding color or retouching thermal dye sublimation prints, for example, as apply to conventional RC (resin-coated) photographic papers. Retouch dyes, which absorb directly into the paper, are excellent for correcting color, spotting blemishes or enhancing certain colors within the image.

Laser color copy output paper, as another example, has a more matte finish than dye-sublimation prints, and, with proper surface preparation, takes pencil coloring well. As with all materials, test how colors blend, how dyes or oils absorb and the best methods for correction on each new type of paper you encounter. The way the color is formed on the print, whether it be thermal or inkjet, can influence the way the added oils and dyes react.

© Grace Schaub

For this color copy paper print, produced from a laser copy machine, a fine coating of Marshall's Pre-Color Spray was applied and allowed to dry before handcoloring. Marshall's pencils dipped in PM Solution were used to lay down areas of color, which were blended with #000 to #2 brushes. Oils were also applied with a paintbrush and cotton. Extender was used to thin out color in select areas. Details were cleaned out with a very sharp pencil, followed by blending with a #000 brush. Note: Marlene applied to an unsprayed color copyprint will result in removing the dye from the print.

Palm Springs Life

California's Prestige Magazine

SEPTEMBER 1990/ TEN DOLLA

Annual Desert Living Issue
1990/1991

Marketing Handcolored Images

Throughout this Guide, there are many examples of how artists have marketed their handcolored images. Some sell their work as illustrations, used on magazine covers, postcards and posters, while others work in fine arts, or sell at arts and crafts fairs. Others do portraiture which they handcolor, or work as artists in handcoloring studios dedicated to serving portrait photographers. In each case, the artists have put in long and hard hours developing a style or approach, a portfolio of representative work and a group of clients who choose to use handcoloring because of the distinct and unique flavor it lends to images.

In a sense, handcoloring is another creative tool available to all photographers, one that adds a special touch to images. As such, it is very popular with greeting card, calendar and poster publishing companies. A number of artists featured in this guide—including Thea Schrack, Jill Enfield, Cheryl Winser and others—have had greeting cards, posters and calendars published by major publishers.

For this market, putting together a portfolio of work, including various themes and unique images—is key. Once a set of images has been completed, make very good quality copy slides of them to be used as your "calling cards." Contact the publishing company (whose address usually appears on the card or calendar, or is available through photographers' marketing books) for their submission guidelines. Follow the guidelines closely (for example, you may be asked to submit a series of shots for a calendar with a "Beach" theme, or potential images for greeting cards for a specific holiday.)

The unique rendition of handcoloring is also popular for illustrations used on book covers, magazine covers, advertisements and even CD covers. Handcoloring adds a special mood and emotion that appeals to many tastes, and is versatile enough to cover a wide variety of illustration needs.

Artists such as Rita Dibert, Pamela and Phillip Lawson, Barbara Leven and Karen Schulman, among many others in this Guide, are active in this field. While some may feel color-by-computer may eliminate handcoloring as a commercial illustration tool, most agree with the statement made by writer Jane Conner Ziser in an article in Photo Electronic Imaging Magazine: "Of all the special effects the computer is capable of reproducing, it's not able to duplicate the style, texture and "feel" of a beautifully painted photographic oil." And with the surge of black-and-white photography in the advertising market, the visibility of handcoloring has increased as well.

As with any marketing, a well thought-out portfolio is key to success in the illustration market. Visiting advertising agencies, public relations agencies and other picture buyers and assigners of work is key. Many artists in this book work for agencies as handcolorists for other photographers' work, and often work on old pictures which have to be colorized. Once the agency is familiar with the talents and focus of an artist, they will keep that artist's name on file for future work.

While the fine art market is probably the most difficult to "crack", quite a few photographers in this Guide show their work regularly in galleries, and sell their work to collectors, museums and corporations. Once again, a portfolio is the main vehicle of showing work, as are very good copy slides.

There's also the "stock" market, an open-ended library where buyers seek a very wide variety of images for various uses. Here, handcoloring is also found, as evidenced by photographers and handcolorists Jill Enfield, Michael Gesinger and Deborah Gilbert. Deborah Gilbert and Jill Enfield's handcolored images are available for sale through the Image Bank, a worldwide stock agency.

As you read through the gallery section, you'll see that virtually every artist featured has been involved with marketing their handcoloring, whether it be through selling individual images, selling rights to the image for illustrations or paper products, or working as a handcolorist for their own or another photographer's portraits.

Gallery

Featuring the handcolored images and techniques of the following artists:

PAULA BOAM

TERENCE CHUA

SANDRA RUSSELL CLARK

NORM DARWISH

MEHOSH DZIADZIO

RITA DIBERT

JILL ENFIELD

RENA BASS FORMAN

KATHLEEN FRANCOUR

MICHAEL GESINGER

DEBORAH GILBERT

MARSHA POLIER GROSSMAN

NORA HERNANDEZ

COLLEEN KENYON

PAMELA & PHILLIP LAWSON

BARBARA LEVEN

PEGGY LINDT

GAIL MATSUI

GREG MacGREGOR

JENNIFER McCLINTOCK

HOWARD MICHAELS

BOB PERRIN

AIMÉE PORTER & ALICE BRUCE

RICHARD PREHN

VICTORIA RYAN

GEORGE SCHAUB

THEA SCHRACK

KAREN SCHULMAN

PAT SMITH & ELSIE MOLTZ (COLORTONE)

DAN SPAHN

SAM SWANLUND

CURTICE TAYLOR

TRACIE TAYLOR

ALLAN TEGER

ANNA TOMCZAK

LINDA WEAVER

JO WHALEY

CHERYL WINSER

ANTHONY YAZZOLINO

© Peggy Lindt, Point Blank Design

LINDA WEAVER

Linda Weaver is a nationally-recognized photographer and handcoloring artist. She has exhibited, judged and lectured throughout the United States and Europe, and has received numerous awards, including the Eastman Kodak Gallery of Excellence Award, the Professional Photographers of America Master Artist Degree and the American Photographic Artisans Guild Laurel Degree, among others. Linda Weaver's Studio is maintained in a restored cattle shed on the scenic former estate of R.J. Reynolds in Winston-Salem, North Carolina. The studio includes a gallery, painting studio, camera room and photographic darkroom.

Linda Weaver Studios has become known for the skill and artistry brought to their client's work. Says Weaver, "Since the work (often involving restoration and handcoloring) is very exacting, most orders will take anywhere from six to twelve weeks to complete. However, some orders take longer; that's because I'm sometimes given very little to work with...I've had to put family portraits together from all sorts of individual pictures...I've used driver's licenses and even newspaper clippings to create a likeness."

Even basic restorations don't go entirely without the use of oil paint, notes Weaver. "I use it to change the density of an area and apply it with cotton. To eliminate areas, such as backgrounds, it is applied with brushes."

Weaver's tips on technique are described in the step-by-step portrait on pages 28 and 29. Her work continues a long tradition of handcoloring mastery, one that is appreciated by her clients. In fact, her studio draws interest as well as work. "I have a painting room adjacent to my gallery with french doors leading into it and a large window on the courtyard. People will often stop by and watch me paint."

Photo Courtesy: Linda Weaver; handcoloring: Linda Weaver

Photos courtesy: Linda Weaver;
handcoloring: Linda Weaver.
For Linda Weaver's step-by-step techniques,
28-29.

Kathleen Francour

Kathleen Francour worked as a model for over a dozen years, then turned her attention to the other side of the camera. She turned her garage into a studio, and began doing head shots and portfolios for other models and actors. Her career in handcoloring began with a chance meeting. As she relates it, "I was having lunch with my three-year old son and a friend at a restaurant one day, and a woman named Paula Boam walked up to our table and handed me a charming hand-tinted greeting card featuring two children."

Boam inquired about using Francour's child as a model, and a relationship began that resulted in Boam trading training in handcoloring for modeling fees for Francour's child. Says Francour, "Thus was my introduction to handtinting. I will always be grateful to Paula. Her generosity of spirit changed the course of my life forever and began my journey back to art." (Boam's work is shown later in this book.)

Francour is drawn to children as her subjects. As she says, "There is no expression so spontaneously pure as that of a young child. In my opinion, the pastel hand tinting of black-and-white photographs especially compliments children in a way that color film seldom does. It enhances the soft innocence of the child in a timeless and often whimsical way."

Francour's work has appeared on many paper products and in many publications, including over 700 greeting cards, dozens of posters and art prints and in children's fashion catalogs. She is the featured artist for the 1995 Children's Hour calendar, as well as the 1996 Earth Angels calendar, both published by Portal Press.

"Unlike most handtinting artists," she says, "I do not use a matte surface paper. I prefer a smooth surface on papers from Oriental Seagull or Ilford Galerie. I generally don't tone my prints. I like the pastel look I get with cool b&w papers. Occasionally I will do a light golden sepia toning as I did with my angel series. Printing is an art in itself and is not my area of expertise." Francour uses Isgo Lepejian Custom B&W Labs, or Philip Narduli or Olson Color Expressions for very large of special-toned prints.

"Because I use a smooth surface paper I don't have to prep the surface...nor do I use Marlene, Extender or an eraser to clean off unwanted paint. A cotton swab wipes it right off. I sometimes use Marlene for a final cleanup around the borders. I apply paint sparingly with cotton swabs, fingertips and tiny fine-point or flat-edged paint brushes. I buff the color smooth with 100% cotton balls.

Photography and handtinting by Kathleen Francour © 1994

"Since the paper has no tooth to it, it doesn't grab the color like matte paper and it takes slightly longer to dry (around three days.) Because the oils just lay on the surface it is also easily scratched even after it is dry, so a matte spray should be applied to the dry print for protection."

Says Francour about her work, "We all have memories from our childhoods, tucked away in the quietest corners of our hearts that have helped shape the adults we have become. These memories will sometimes spill into our present day thoughts and bring a smile, or even a tear as we reflect on times past and old dreams forgotten. I try to create images that tap into these feelings and evoke an emotional response."

PAULA BOAM

In 1983, Paula Boam took a picture of her four year old daughter in black and white. Says Boam, "It was beautiful, but it lacked something. I began to look at old photos that had been handcolored and that led me to used book stores and finally an old copy of 'Photo Oil Coloring' (by Lucile Marshall.) The result was so unique that I began submitting photos to various companies.

"Terragrafics, a frame company, loved the look and bought over 200 of my images. I went on to do 48 greeting cards for Michael & Co. and four posters for Bernard & Co. This last year Kaplan did four more posters, and recently I did a greeting card for Marcel Schurman."

Boam's work uses classic handcoloring techniques, applied with a special style. However, she also believes in freeing creative energy through experimentation—a case in point is her "children running" image, shown here.

"The technique I used for the children running was really learned by trial and error. After I had printed the picture I felt the background was distracting. In my darkroom was a container of bleach, so I took the picture, still wet, from the fix and applied the bleach to areas I no longer wanted with a cotton swab. As I was doing this, I was also running water over the picture surface so that the bleach wouldn't be too strong in any one area.

"That didn't work out exactly the way I had planned. The finished dry photo was raw in some places with emulsion left in others. I decided to paint it anyway. The result, to me, was exciting. The colors took differently everywhere. Since the picture was becoming something very far from my usual style, I decided to keep it going. I then added the oils heavier on the children's clothes and hair with a spot-tone brush.

"After doing this print, I was able to go back to my original style with something very valuable. That was the technique of using the spot-tone brush with oils. I have since created flowers and wreaths, added lace and details to many things using this method. I have used 'dotting' many times since. Dotting is simply putting little white dots all around your subject.

"The best thing you can do as an artist/photographer is let your creative energy free. After all, you will always have the original negative, and a new print is just three trays away."

NORA HERNANDEZ

Nora Hernandez was always interested in photography, and after her first child was born she became more involved. She took a photography class in a local high school, and learned many of the darkroom techniques she still employs today. Later, she met a neighbor, Paula Boam, who was also working with photography and her children. They began experimenting with tinting photos.

Hernandez now has a fulltime business, Bonnets & Lace, specializing in hand-tinted photographs of children. She also works with a local parent-child magazine as a staff photographer and creates the monthly cover photo. Her work has appeared on many posters, greeting cards and postcards, with clients including Gibson Cards, Argus Communications, M.W. Carr and Amor Image, Paris, France.

Says Hernandez, "Different papers give a different look. Some of my favorite papers are Luminos RCR-ART, Luminos Classic Tapestry X, Kodak Ektalure G and Agfa Portriga Rapid 118. Occasionally I have problems getting the paper to take a tint. When this happens I rub the paper down with Extender, oil or gel before tinting.

On handcoloring tips, Hernandez advises, "Use more than one color on each item, such as clothing. If you want to make a dress pink, use pink for the highlight areas and violet for the shadows. When tinting water, use lots of colors with darker colors for the shadow areas. Use brushes to add detail.

"It is important to balance color throughout the picture. Don't overuse one color unless you specifically want to bring focus to one area, such as with commercial work...To save paint, store your work palettes with paint on them in the freezer. I've saved plenty doing this."

© Nora Hernandez

AIMÉE PORTER AND ALICE BRUCE

Aimée Porter and Alice Bruce, a mother-daughter team, have had their work published in magazines and on greeting cards and calendars. The photographer side of the team, Aimée Porter has always loved working with children, and she has become well known for her work photographing children of diverse races and backgrounds. Alice Bruce has loved and studied art for most of her life. Her experience using both oil and watercolor has given her a very strong foundation for her handcoloring technique. In addition to their work for publication they have a portrait business.

Says Alice Bruce, whose handcoloring so finely matches Aimée Porter's delightful photography, "Using a fiber-based paper I apply Marshall's oils with facial tissue. I dislike the feel of cotton and like the results and greater control I achieve using this method. I believe that the magic happens in handtinting when three colors are next to each other; until there are three colors working together I know that my picture hasn't reached full potential.

"This is especially true with the details in the photograph, such as flowers, leaves, clothing patterns, etc. An invaluable tool has been an eraser that can be sharpened. This can be especially effective in highlighting eye whites, teeth, ruffles, flower petals, etc. Like most handtinters, I find that pencils are best used to bring out or highlight strands of hair, eyes, lips, veins on leaves, tree branches and flower petals."

Peggy Lindt

As a teenager, Peggy Lindt began selling her paintings and illustrations in galleries in Mendocino, California. She completed her education in illustration and design at Otis Art Institute in Los Angeles and at Parsons School of Design in New York, and began a career in commercial art. She is the winner of many awards, including a Gold Medal in poster design from the American Institute of Graphic Artists, and Ad Club competitions in Southern California. Her editorial and cover illustrations have appeared in Santa Barbara Magazine, the Los Angeles Times and other national magazines. She has been handcoloring since 1983, either her own photography or vintage images from a variety of sources. She is currently working on posters, notecards, postcards, book jackets, CD covers, calendars and other projects.

Says Lindt, "My background is illustration, so I approach every image as a painting, with detail in mind. In handtinting, I try to balance the choice and intensity of color to the mood and message of the photograph, maintaining the integrity of the original black-and-white image.

"The Wedding Group handtinted photograph is a vintage image from circa 1900, found by researching photography collections. The original photograph was badly spotted due to age, so I used a bleach solution and applied it as a wash, mainly to the background. I used the bleach to reduce the intensity of spots and flaws, but didn't try to completely perfect the picture. The result is an enhanced image which still retains its vintage, surreal qualities.

"The print is on Ilford Galerie paper. Then, of course, Marshall's Oils and Pencils were applied. It has been published as a greeting card and appeared as a cover for the national trade magazine "Flowers &".

Sam Swanlund

Sam Swanlund loves the study of history, and combines his gifts as an artist with this love to recreate historical scenes in vivid color paintings. His work is in corporate and personal collections.

Working in his fully-equipped log cabin studio in Eureka, California, he begins with glass plate negatives that are about 100 years old. He makes prints that vary in size from 2x3-feet to 3x4-feet. He then mounts the prints on Gatorboard, does his research and paints with Marshall's Photo Oils. The original handcolored paintings are then photographed, and 16x20 Cibachromes (now Ilfochrome Classic) are made after the original work is sold.

Handcoloring by Peggy Lindt.
Black-and-White Photo Courtesy of Santa Barbara Historical Museums.

Handcoloring by Sam Swanlund.

COLORTONE ARTISTS

Colortone Artists is an independently owned establishment dedicated to special techniques for photographic art. Owned and operated by Pat Smith, Colortone is respected throughout the photographic community for both the high quality of their work and the individual attention each piece receives. Pat Smith started with Colortone in 1954, and learned her craft from the original proprietor, Sid Coner.

For years, the establishment was exclusively devoted to hand coloring. Now Colortone Artists offer both restoration and direct retouching services as well. The area of specialization remains in the family and personal photo business. They work with photographers and studios all across the United States in "correcting" direct color prints, as well as heavy oil coloring for large-scale presentation portraits. Their work in photographic restoration was featured on CBS television in 1987.

All work that comes from Colortone Artists is personally attended to by Smith and her employee, Elsie Moltz. Pat Smith has 40 years of handcoloring experience, and Elsie Moltz has almost 30 years to her credit. Smith believes that hand coloring and restoration help keep precious memories alive for all of Colortone's clientele. "It's a wonderful feeling knowing our handiwork helps keep people's memories alive for many, many generations to come."

Often, photos arrive damaged or torn. After a careful restoration, the handcoloring work begins. For the woman's portrait here, the background was created with Marshall's Sky Blue with a touch of Neutral and Extender; after blending, a touch of Cheek and Raw Sienna was added. This was then blended with cotton to a smooth tone.

For the skintone, Marshall's Basic Flesh served as the foundation, with Venetian Red added to the cheeks. After a smooth blending, a clean cotton-tipped skewer was used to rub down all highlight areas. For the shadow areas, Venetian Red and Burnt Umber were applied and blended.

The lips also received Venetian Red. The hair color results from Burnt Umber, with careful attention to blending down all highlight areas for sheen.

For the eyebrows, Burnt Umber, with soft blending, creates a beautiful effect. After color is added to the eyes, the whites are cleared carefully, and a touch of white is added to the button of the eye to create a highlight. The jewelry is colored with Burnt Sienna, while the dress is colored with Sky Blue with a touch of Viridian.

While color and blending for the woman's portrait was done with skewers and cotton, a different approach, working with brushes for paint application, was used for the portrait of the bride and groom. This technique can be more exacting, yet with detail comes more demands. Often, brush application is used for details after cotton application and blending has been done first.

Though the portrait of the bride and groom was damaged, there was no pre-coloring restoration work done. All damage was covered by the application of paint on the copy print. While this may work for sections or slightly damaged originals, heavily damaged originals, such as the woman's portrait, will need to go through the copy/restore/copy cycle before coloring is begun.

The fleshtone here is a mixture of White, Raw Sienna, Crimson and a touch of Burnt Umber. The bride's dress was covered with White, with shadow details provided by Raw Sienna and a touch of Neutral. The flowers are colored by Carmine and White. The man's suit is simple Black, with some highlights provided by clearing paint.

A good deal of restoration was needed on the back of the chair, and the details here were created using Verona Brown, Raw Sienna and Sepia. The backdrop was painted with Verona Brown and Crimson.

The quality and care seen in the work of the Colortone Artists, Smith and Moltz, are clearly part of the finest tradition of studio artists who have been helping preserve treasured family memories ever since the first days of photography.

*Restoration and handcoloring
by Colortone Artists.*

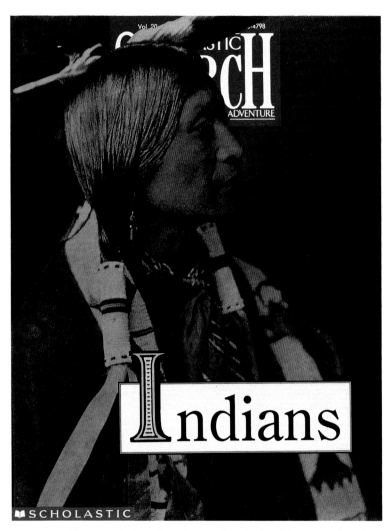

Photography by Edward Curtis, handcolored by Howard Michaels, reprinted with the permission of Scholastic Magazine. January, 1992 issue.

HOWARD MICHAELS

Howard Michaels' handcoloring work includes a wide range of subject matter, using images from the turn of the century and early 1950's family snapshots as source material. He is best known for scenes of New Jersey coastal towns made in the early twentieth century. He has self-published two books, "Victorian Holidays" and "Self-Guided Architectural Tours of Cape May, New Jersey." His handcoloring work has appeared in Scholastic Magazine, Victorian Homes Magazine and the Princeton University Alumni Magazine.

Says Michaels, "As an artist who hand paints black-and-white photographs, I look for images that have a nostalgic appeal and tonal quality that allows me to meticulously work on details. I almost always start with a sepia-toned fiber-base print that is usually 11x14-inches. It is best to spend some time analyzing the black-and-white image before applying the paint, but this could sometimes be a luxury.

"A case in point is the Scholastic Magazine cover portrait of the Native American, taken by photographer Edward Curtis early in the twentieth century. With a deadline of three days to receive, complete and send back to New York City, there was no time for contemplation. A special warm quality was achieved by using mainly earth tones and shades of primary colors for contrast. For the last detail, oil pencils were used to apply the blue and yellow highlights on the jet black hair. I always use a clear gloss lacquer to finish and protect the work.

"In the handcoloring of the railroad at Barnegat Light, New Jersey (circa 1910) the painterly application of oils on the dunes and lighthouse was done purposely to separate the action from the serenity of the scene."

Handpainted by Howard Michaels, 1991.

TERENCE CHUA

Terence Chua is a software designer who holds a degree in Physics and a Masters in Computer Science. He began handcoloring in 1984, and at first duplicated what could be obtained with color film. He then decided that the use of the oils provided him the opportunity to render an "alternate point of view," with the stated aim of attracting the viewer's eye.

His use of bright, sometimes discordant colors began from what could be described as a creative accident. While handcoloring, he squeezed out more purple than needed from a tube. As he says, "Well, I had to use all this oil somewhere, and that somewhere turned out to be a purple-colored building. From then on I started experimenting with mixing my own colors to get the mood and the strength."

He prefers to print his own images, and prints about 1/3 stop lighter than normal. He processes his paper to archival standards, and uses toner to give the print a brownish base color.

Says Chua, "I mix colors when needed. I use Marshall's Extender quite a bit to get varying shades of a tint. And when detail is not required, or a pastel-like effect is wanted, I mix white with the other tints. The main thing is that art is a process of discovering new things! It is exciting! So instead of wondering what an image will look like in a particular shade, just try it.

"I remind myself that the most important thing when applying color is that removing the unwanted color is as important as applying the colors retained."

© 1989 T. Chua

THEA SCHRACK

Thea Schrack studied commercial photography at Colorado Mountain College and received a BFA at the San Francisco Art Institute in 1983. Currently a freelance photographer in San Francisco, she has had many shows on the West Coast, as well as a one-person show of her hand-colored photographs in Switzerland in 1994. In 1987 she was chosen as one of the New Faces in Fine Art by American Photographer Magazine. Along with her fine art work Schrack works commercially for advertising, editorial and fashion clients, and has of late been creating covers for various recording companies.

Schrack photographs with many different cameras, including a Widelux (panorama camera)

used for the "Shadow of Time" landscape here. In many instances, she sepia tones the print prior to handcoloring.

Says Schrack, "My coloring technique is very traditional. I apply P.M. Solution, wipe the print dry and apply Marshall's Oils with cotton. I often do a lot of mixing of all the different colors to broaden my range, especially for the range of subtle colors."

Schrack's work appears on greeting cards (Palm Press and Pomegranate Press) and on album covers (Sony Music CDs.) She also does work for the National Park Service, handcoloring historic photographs.

Rena Bass Forman

Rena Bass Forman received her B.A. in Art History from Hofstra University in 1975, and a degree in Arts Administration/Creative Arts in Education from Rutgers University in 1979. Her work has appeared in numerous group and solo shows. Forman's landscapes are characterized by a subtlety of tone and an emotional response to a sense of place.

Says Forman, "I never take a color photograph to help me remember the way a landscape looked. I rely solely on my inner sense of memory...I revert back to the place within myself that allows me to recapture the mood and quality of light...The layering of painting and photography presents particular technical challenges and I always begin at the top of a photograph and work my way down.

"I usually approach the skies in quite a painterly way, using many colors layered upon one another, first blending them on the palette and then on the print itself. I know the color is right for me when I begin to see the magic that prompted me to take the photograph in the first place. I then spend a great deal of time going back in, making adjustments and reworking the colors. Highlighting with accent colors is always the last step, and I often accomplish this with oil pastels and pencils. I strive towards a subtle richness in my colors that allows itself to shed a mysterious light on my subject."

Forman has several tips to share: "Choose the right paper...My favorite is Kodak Ektalure G. I love the texture and creamy quality... I know if I want an image to be full of golden tones I usually begin with a sepia-toned print. If I want to use blues I might use a selenium toner or stick with an untoned print. I never pre-coat the prints unless I am working on a paper that holds on to the paint making it difficult to blend. I use either wax paper or marble palettes, placing an array of colors out at first, blending them to get the right tones, using neutral tint to dim the brightness.

"For skies I often use a great deal of Titanium White under and over other colors for a highlight effect. I save the clouds for last, careful to clean my edges as I go along."

© Rena Bass Forman

BOB PERRIN

The authors first saw Bob Perrin's work in a photo gallery while walking down the main street of Nevada City in Northern California. Says Perrin, "I am a fine arts photographer currently showing my black-and-white and handcolored limited-edition prints in selected galleries and shows in the 'Gold Country' of Northern California.

"My procedure is to first lightly sepia tone the matte-finish print, changing the lighter shades of grays to tans and browns; the darker tones remain almost unchanged. Then, Marshall's Photo Oils are applied with the basic cotton swab and cotton ball technique. Detail and color highlight punch are added with small art brushes and Marshall's Photo Pencils. When complete, my work will look more like an oil painting than a photograph."

© Bob Perrin

GEORGE SCHAUB

Co-author of this guide, George Schaub has been handcoloring since 1970. He has exhibited widely, and has had numerous articles published on handcoloring. Schaub's father was a professional photographer and lab technician, whose portrait studio used the services of a handcoloring artist. Schaub's work has been geared more toward landscape and experimental uses of color. He works with Marshall's Oils, Pencils and Retouch Colors.

Says Schaub, "As most of my earlier work in photography was strictly in black-and-white, handcoloring became a natural outlet for any desire for color imagery. Later, when I began shooting more color, handcoloring became a way of dealing with color abstraction, and was used in conjunction with metallic toning, alternative printing techniques and solarization. The surreal quality of color becomes even more so when the photographer can control how that color dominates, or whispers in the image.

"I work in a fairly straightforward fashion, printing on warm-toned fiber-based papers and applying the colors with a cotton swab or brush, as required. I have found that working with pencils in conjunction with oils is an excellent way to control highlights and add touches of color to minute areas. I often use the Retouch Colors to enhance conventional colorprints, especially in highlight areas. I'll have a few sets of a print made and experiment 'til it looks right."

© George Schaub

JILL ENFIELD

Jill Enfield's work is in galleries and permanent collections throughout the U.S. and abroad. She has been actively exhibiting her work for more than a decade, and her hand-colored images have appeared on posters and notecards as well. She has taught handcoloring workshops, and is a member of the faculty at Parsons School of Design in New York. Her handcoloring work has also been used for commercial and editorial work, with clients including Vassarette Lingerie, AT&T, Con Edison, American Way Magazine and American Heritage Magazine.

Enfield works primarily with infrared black-and-white film. For this image, she printed on Kodak Ektalure G paper. Says Enfield, "I do not prepare the print with P.M. Solution before I paint. I first attach the print to a piece of mat-board easel that I also use as a blotter. Using oil paints and pencils, I mix my colors on a palette and apply them on to the print with a toothpick.

Then I take a wad of cotton and move the paint around the print.

"I do not try to stay in the lines at this stage because I get more of an even coat by spreading it over a large area. I then use P.M. Solution or turpenoid to get the paint off. I dip a cotton swab into the turpenoid, dab it onto the mat board and then start removing the unwanted color. I use a dry cotton swab and my fingers to go back over the area to get off the excess liquid, changing the cotton swab often so it keeps removing paint.

"On this particular print I first applied the blue to the building and then orange to selected areas. To make the two tones look blended I took one of the pieces of cotton used for blending the blue and rubbed it gently on top of the orange. This alleviates the problem of staying in the lines by softening the edges where the two colors meet. The roof was done by taking different color pencils and drawing with all of them and blending them together at one time."

CURTICE TAYLOR

Curtice Taylor has been handcoloring for fifteen years. In addition to his work for collectors and galleries, he is active in handcoloring for book jackets, magazine articles and record albums. Some clients include New York Magazine, Art & Antiques Magazine and the New York Times Magazine. His fine art work incorporates several major themes, including "Renaissance-style" nudes, 1950's American cars and ruins in Italy. He generally paints over the entire surface, and his work is characterized by strong color.

Says Taylor, "The techniques of handcoloring aren't very difficult, but thinking like a painter does not come easily to many photographers. You must let the underlying b&w image be your guide. It lets you know where there are highlights and shadows.

"It is difficult to paint over black, but dark gray shadows can have color added. Conversely, white areas look flat when painted, but light gray areas have some structure to support a highlight color like yellow. It is best to use a medium-contrast print that is a little on the light side.

"Certainly, the more graphic the picture the better. Photographs with many trees or flowers are going to be a daunting task...larger prints are often easier to paint than small ones. 5x7-inch prints limit your choices and force you to work in minute detail. 11x14-inch is a good size."

SANDRA RUSSELL CLARK

Sandra Russell Clark is a native of New Orleans, where she is well known for her infrared and hand-colored photography of Louisiana landscapes and European and American gardens. Her work has been exhibited widely, and she has also had her work published in a variety of magazines, including Vogue, Mirabella, American Artist and New Orleans magazine. Her images are in the collections of many corporations and museums, as well as important private collections.

Along with having been a curator and professor of photography, she now teaches private photography and handcoloring workshops in the U.S. and abroad. She is currently working on a book entitled "Venice, a Vanishing Light."

All her work is photographed on infrared film, printed on Agfa Portriga Rapid fiber base paper, brown toned and handcolored with Marshall's Oils. Says Clark, "Because of the subject matter, image size and depth is important to me. I prefer printing 16x20 to 30x40 inches, and I select a glossy surface to create more depth in the landscape.

"The paper is coated with P.M. Solution and then wiped down. The colors are applied with toothpicks and cotton very sparsely to related areas...The paint is used to create contrast and a surreal effect, which gives the viewer a sense of a world in between reality and dreams."

DAN SPAHN

A graduate of Northern Illinois University with an M.A. in Studio Art, Dan Spahn works as a freelance photographer and handcolorist. He has exhibited in both group and solo shows (including a show at the University of Delaware in 1989) and has his work in universities, art museums and corporate collections throughout the country. His current and ongoing project involves handcolored photographs of gardens and architecture in Chicago and Palm Beach, Florida.

Spahn prints his images on Kodak G (textured) surface paper, and processes all his images according to archival standards. In addition, all prints are sepia-toned, which both converts the silver image to a more stable form and provides an image color base that is conducive to handcoloring. Spahn uses cotton swabs to apply his paint, and long fiber cotton for blending. Details are painted with cotton wrapped around toothpicks, or with Marshall's Pencils.

Says Spahn, "Until very recently handcoloring was the only permanent color image commonly available to the public. And although great advances have been made in color photographic materials the handcolored photograph has the longest known stability in color photographic image permanency."

© Curtice Taylor

© Sandra Russell Clark

© Dan Spahn

ANNA TOMCZAK

Anna Tomczak's work in handcoloring began nearly twenty years ago. She received her BA from Penn State University and her MFA from the University of Florida. She has lectured widely and taught workshops on handcoloring at the Palm Beach Photo Workshops, the Southeast Museum of Photography and the University of Art in Philadelphia. Her work has been exhibited widely throughout the United States and Europe, and is in numerous corporate and museum collections.

Says Tomczak about her work, "My method for working with color on silver prints is to integrate the paint into the surface of the paper. This creates a very realistic approach to painting. My imagery is constructed with color in mind, but it is not always previsualized. Very often, the color changes the visual quality of the image, just as it does in any painting. To me, these images are as much painting as they are photography.

"Using found objects (botanicals, memorabilia, artifacts) and altering their meaning through a random juxtaposition, I define a fragment of time. The objects are transferred into an imagined world of their own, frozen in ice, or lit by sparklers, becoming symbols from an unknown civilization."

Commenting on Tomczak's work, Katherine Duncan, Curator of Exhibitions at the Polk Museum of Art said, "Tomczak's images often seem surreal because of the choices she makes when combining object and color. The intensified color creates states of heightened awareness, and in their hypnotic dreaminess they often appear more 'real' than our perception of reality."

© Anna Tomczak

© Anna Tomczak

DEBORAH GILBERT

Deborah Gilbert says that the credits for the old "Saturday Night Live" program got her interest started in handcoloring. Prior to that, she had studied art privately, and then at the Tyler School of Art. She took up photography, gaining knowledge by working in a small camera shop. However, in 1981, her life took a turn when she applied for and was accepted into the Ringling Brothers & Barnum & Bailey Clown College.

She says that she has currently combined her three loves—photography, painting and clowns—into her art work. She self-published a clown calendar, which was featured in Parade magazine's "buys of the week" section, and she had 4000 orders in one month. She also does photography and handcoloring for stock photography. Once a photo editor at Image Bank, she now does still life and other images for sale as stock around the world. She also teaches a course in stock photography at the Parsons School of Design/New School in New York.

She is currently working on two books—one that she says "captures clowns' souls" and the other about the Muscular Dystrophy Society's Summer Camps.

Says Gilbert, "I print on Kodak Polyfiber, F (glossy) surface, then sepia tone the prints. I spread the paint on the surface with a cotton swab and use cotton wads to smooth the paint and get the desired texture and color saturation. For small areas, I wrap cotton around a toothpick. I also mix colors directly on the image surface. I feel that part of the fun of handcoloring is using 'unexpected' color."

JENNIFER J. McCLINTOCK

Currently residing in San Diego, CA, Jennifer J. McClintock works as a freelance photographer specializing in handcolored portraiture and still life. She became interested in handcoloring as a way of adding a unique touch to her photography. She has had several exhibitions of her work, with her still life images selling as limited editions and for use in greeting cards. She also does commissioned handcolored portraits.

Says McClintock, "All of my photographs are printed on Agfa Portriga Rapid 118 paper. This is a creamy-based, matte surface paper that accepts oils, pencils and dyes exceptionally well. Unless I'm working with dyes, I first treat the surface with Marshall's P.M. Solution, to allow the media to be manipulated and blended easily."

For her image (right) she chose the vase colors first, applied the mixed colors with cotton swabs and emphasized the highlights and shadows with pencils. She usually mixes color on a palette before application.

Says McClintock, "I've found that oils, pencils and dyes work best with my style of photography. I use cotton swabs to apply the color, and blend it with my fingers or loose cotton. I clean off any overlaps with an eraser and Marshall's Marlene solution. I use pencils for form and definition, blending them with cotton swabs. I tend to lean towards realism with my technique, leaving little or no evidence of unblended oils or pencils."

ANTHONY YAZZOLINO

A native Californian, Anthony Yazzolino studied art and design at the Cornish School of Allied Arts in Seattle. His early career was as a graphic artist, but he describes his involvement with photography, begun in 1984, as an "intense passion." His work has been exhibited widely, and is in many private collections. He also teaches handtinting at a local college and via workshops.

Says Yazzolino, "I prefer a darker print with complete details in shadows and highlights. I like to print myself for the obvious reason of having complete control. I have tried virtually every paper and still feel that Agfa Portriga Rapid 118 is the best and most consistent for handcoloring. Generally, when doing portraits I will sepia tone the prints. This is a good base color for a more natural flesh tone.

"Application is relatively easy. Before I tint, I will prepare the paper with P.M. Solution, not too heavy, so it allows me to blend and reduce colors more easily. Of course the image is what really matters. I am not trying to make a color photograph, but to continue the artistic expression that I desire. Color tinting an image allows me to control the color in order to enhance what my vision is."

Finally, Yazzolino quotes from an essay by Therese Heyman on the occasion of an exhibit, "Watkins to Weston, 101 Years of California Photography": "The pictorialist's success may have been overshadowed by that of the generation of photographers that followed them. But in a longer view of photography it may be that manipulation, handcoloring and collage will come to be seen as basic to photographers' artistic expression."

COLLEEN KENYON

Colleen Kenyon graduated from Skidmore College in 1973, and received her MFA from Indiana University in 1976. She has received numerous grants for her work, including the New York Foundation for the Arts Photography Fellowship in 1989. She has exhibited extensively both in the United States and abroad, and has over 85 individual and group shows to her credit, including shows at the Friends of Photography in San Francisco, the Museum of Modern Art in New York, and a show on the Hand Colored Photograph in the Philadelphia College of Art. She has served as curator of numerous shows, given many lectures and has had her work published on cards, posters and in a wide variety of magazines. She is currently Executive Director at the Center for Photography, Woodstock, NY.

Kenyon photographs her work for handcoloring on Kodak Plus-X 35mm film, and prints on semi-matte Kodak Polycontrast N or Agfa Portriga matte paper. The photographs are then sepia toned and painted with Marshall's Oils and Pencils.

In a "Statement on Work" dated January, 1994, Colleen Kenyon wrote:

> *"From light and its twin—*
> *cast shadows—*
> *ambiguity arises*
> *releasing a complexity*
> *of interior messages.*
> *With no actual substance,*
> *light becomes a barricade."*

She also quoted Christina Rossetti, from "A Royal Princess":

> *"All my walls are lost in mirrors,*
> *whereupon I trace*
> *Self to right hand, self to left*
> *hand, self in every place,*
> *Self-same solitary figure, self-same*
> *seeking face."*

PHILLIP AND PAMELA LAWSON

The Lawsons work as a husband and wife team. Their work has appeared in many issues of Palm Springs Life Magazine, and they have designed and created many book covers for St. Martin's Press and Harlequin Books. They have also created numerous movie posters for Turner Broadcasting, and their work is in many corporate and private collections.

Phillip and Pamela Lawson say that they put less emphasis on specific techniques and more on a certain style that they have developed over the past ten years. Though both are knowledgeable in computers, and have been actively working in that medium since 1985, they take pride that their photo illustration work is created "by hand" with handcoloring. Says Pamela Lawson, "Our handcoloring methods are cost effective and time effective. The techniques we use produce a particular style, and the photographic fiber paper output has a very warm appeal for original art or gallery work. Computers can't do everything!

"A good friend of ours, a very well-known movie poster illustrator, noticed his work had slowed down considerably when all the buzz in computer technology was big in the early 90's…However, he again has plenty of work, although he continues to do his illustrations by hand. Perhaps agencies are finally demanding quality and style once again and not settling for so much generic computer art."

The teamwork of creation finds Phillip handling the shooting, printing and darkroom manipulation, and Pamela handling the handcoloring. Pamela says she prefers the look obtained with a thin, smooth coat of paint, rather than through building color on color. Experimentation is key, and there may be a mockup stage where the work is colored with pencils and photocopied before a final color scheme is approved.

MICHAEL GESINGER

Michael Gesinger received his MFA in Photography from the University of Washington in 1978, and has exhibited widely in both group and one-man shows. His work is in the permanent collections of the Portland Art Museum, Pacific Northwest Bell and the Seattle Arts Commission Portable Arts Collection, to name a few. He began toning prints in 1980, and hand-coloring in 1985. Says Gesinger, "Color makes such a dramatic change in a print and the control of color is a wonderful freedom. Each print becomes unique."

Both prints here, "Twisted Nude on a Chaise Lounge" (bottom) and "Nude on White Ledge" were printed on Oriental Portrait Paper. "Twisted Nude" was printed on the Luster surface paper, while "Nude" was printed on a semi-matte surface. Both prints were selenium toned prior to coloring.

"Twisted Nude" was colored with both Marshall's Pencils and Oils. The pencils were used for some of the detail work, such as the trees outside the window, the ceramic flowers on the planter, the base of the wall light and the band bordering the fabric of the couch. For "Nude" only the figure is colored using Marshall's Oils.

Says Gesinger, "I find a semi-matte surface generally the best to work on as it allows use of both oils and pencils. I use Oriental Portrait Luster and Matte surfaces, and Agfa Portriga. Sometimes I use the glossy surface when I plan to color minimally. I always air dry prints. The Agfa paper does not dry to a high gloss and it is quite possible to color it.

"I always selenium tone prints. This primarily changes the base tone of the paper from slightly green to slightly brown—the whites remain essentially white. This base color effects the finished color after oils are applied.

"I seldom use cotton swabs to apply oils or smooth the color. I prefer to roll my own swabs using the wooden skewers provided in the Marshall's kits and long fiber cotton.

"I am not interested in art as a separate, distinct activity, but rather as a process and a manifestation of a unique perspective. My task is to find a path that leads to the source that is me, to tap into that source and to make photographs that reflect it."

CHERYL WINSER

Cheryl Winser had been working as a designer and illustrator when she became interested in handcoloring photographs as a fine art medium. Much later, she happened to be doing handcoloring work for another photographer, and that led to more commercial work. Today, she does a substantial amount of work in collaboration with other photographers and their clients, in addition to shooting and handcoloring her own photographs for various clients. She has been published by Hallmark Cards, Step-by-Step Magazine and Darkroom Techniques Magazine, and her handcoloring has been used in conjunction with other photographers' images for Chicago Magazine, McDonald's Corporation, Sears, RCA Records, Midway Airlines and the Museum of Science and Industry, among many others. Winser also teaches workshops in handcoloring technique.

Winser says that she does not have one favorite paper for handcoloring, as each of the matte or semi-matte surfaces on the market has characteristics that make them appropriate for different types of handcoloring. She does prefer to sepia tone her personal prints.

Says Winser, "I use cotton swabs, as well as cotton-wrapped sticks and toothpicks to apply the oil, and cotton balls to smooth and blend the colors. To clean up large areas I use Marlene, but often on small areas I'll use a white plastic eraser.

"I rarely use the P.M. Solution though it can be useful in some commercial applications. Sometimes I will receive a print that does require some surface preparation. I do enjoy mixing media, but I usually start coloring with Marshall's Oils and then work with pencils over the oils. The extra-strength colors are terrific when you really want a strong color but still want it to be transparent. I do sometimes use oil pastel sticks for finishing touches on a print, and I like to mix handcoloring with collage and drawing."

© Cheryl Winser

© Cheryl Winser

MARSHA POLIER GROSSMAN

Marsha Polier Grossman graduated from the School of the Arts, Virginia Commonwealth University in 1972 with a BFA in Communication Arts and Design. She works as a freelance photograper and specializes in handcoloring her own photographs as well as those supplied by various agencies. She also handcolors engravings. Her work is available as stock photographs. She is represented by Pacific Press Services in Japan and Korea and by Agenzia Fotografica in Italy. She is a member of the studio faculty artists of the Virginia Museum of Fine Arts. Her work includes commercial, editorial and fine art applications of handcoloring. She has been published widely, and has greeting card, CD covers (Time-Life Music Rhythm & Blues series) and various magazine covers and features to her credit.

© 1985 Marsha Polier Grossman

Says Grossman, "I like to work on matte-finish fiber-based paper. I work on sizes ranging from 1-inch square formats used in jewelry to 4 x 6-feet mural size. I print with a soft contrast and will often brown tone the image before handcoloring. For tiny details such as fabric patterns, leaves and small creatures I use liquid dyes applied with small water-color brushes.

"Oils and colored pencils are used especially in medium to large areas and for skintones. My photographs take from one to ten hours to color, and I prefer to work in natural light.

"I begin with liquid dyes and end up with oils and pencil. I rarely pre-coat the entire print with P.M. Solution. I will sometimes apply it to small areas when I am using mainly pencils. I will often dip the pencil into P.M. Solution just before touching the print. I mix many of my own colors from the basic colors supplied by Marshall's Hobby Set.

"Working with liquid dyes is an 'additive process' and working with oils is a 'subtractive process.' With the dyes, I am adding color bit by bit until I achieve the desired color density. With the oils, I am subtracting the color (buffing it) until the desired colors and intensities are achieved. I particularly enjoy working the detailed areas, and my work often reflects a unique variety of depth, tones and intensities because of my willingness to spend hours obsessing on minutiae."

VICTORIA RYAN

New Orleans-based Victoria Ryan, who sells her fine art work through galleries, photographs her work with an 8x10 camera, then uses the negatives to make palladium prints on hand-coated parchment paper. Her first step in hand-coloring is to use Marshall's black and white pencils to enhance the highlights and shadows on the entire print. She then layers colors, working on one section at a time, and blends colors with a cotton swab.

When finished she smooths out the texture using black and white pencils once again. Says Ryan, "Although each print takes a signifigant amount of time, I appreciate the rich tones and texture that I can coax out of the prints."

Ryan's technique is similar when working on silver-gelatin paper. She uses Agfa Portriga 118 paper, as she feels it takes to handcoloring very well without the use of resurfacing sprays. She uses the black and white pencils to touch up detail, then blends the different color values to push up what she calls the "snap" in the print.

© Victoria Ryan

GAIL MATSUI

After attending San Joaquin Delta College and Art Center College of Design, California-based photographer Gail Matsui earned the title of Certified Professional Photographer and began her business in 1992. She uses handcoloring with both Polaroid image transfer and black-and-white infrared photographs.

Using a Vivitar Instant Printer to transfer slides to Polaroid Type 669 film, Matsui then transfers the image onto Arches hot press paper. She then applies a coat of Extender over the entire image, as, she says, "It controls the saturation of the color and the finished texture of the work." It also assures, says Matsui, that the print surface maintains a consistent reflective quality.

In this award-winning image, Titanium White is used to build highlights, with detail color added with Marshall's Pencils. Clean cotton swabs are used for blending.

As to advice, Matsui counsels, "It's important to let the handcolored work dry long enough in a clean, dust-free container with some air circulating over it. I use the Marshall's Pencils a lot because the sharpened point can apply color to very detailed areas. Be patient and practice, practice, practice, because great success often comes from what at first glance appears to be a miserable failure." And, "Handcoloring has helped distinguish my photography as exclusive, one-of-a-kind works of art, and has given me a reputation for meticulous work."

BARBARA LEVEN

Barbara Leven received her BA degree, cum laude, from Queens College, where she majored in Fine Art. Shortly after graduation she turned her attention to photography, and now works in freelance Advertising, People and Portrait photography and as a "Computographer". Clients include Saloman Brothers, ANA Airlines, NEC, the NY Yankees, Time-Warner and Key Pharmaceuticals. Her work is in the permanent collections of the NY Metropolitan Museum of Art and the Cincinnati Art Museum. She has had numerous solo and group shows, has been published widely and has recieved many praiseworthy reviews of her work. She has been using Marshall's Photo Oils since 1978.

Says Leven, "Using my training in fine art oil painting as a base, I developed a technique for Marshall's involving the layering of colors one over the other while the paint is still wet. The transparency of the paint is what allows not only the photography to show through in all its detail, but allows one layer of color to affect what is applied over it to create depth of tone. One example is to apply cadmium yellow over flesh tones in highlight areas to further bring out the three-dimensional quality of the form.

"I have also used Marshall's in both opaque and transparent modes for differing effects. In order to create these varying effects I use cotton swabs, cotton balls and small paintbrushes. The cotton balls and swabs are used to apply the paint evenly, without visible strokes. Paintbrushes are used for heavier paint or where a texture of brushstrokes are desired, or for small, delicate areas such as eyes and lips."

KAREN SCHULMAN

Karen Schulman has studied at the University of California, Los Angeles, and the Otis Art Institute; she has a Masters of Arts in Teaching from Manhattanville College in New York. Her handcoloring work has been used widely by commercial clients, including Agfa Corporation, Miles Communications and Location Update Magazine. She has had greeting cards published by Portal Publications, and has had her work published in a wide range of magazines and video box covers. Her work has been widely exhibited as well. Currently she is working on growing her company, known as Focus Adventures, with an emphasis on the Art of Seeing photo workshops and photo tours.

Says Schulman, "I love to handcolor my favorite images. I am able to personalize it by altering the colors and adding textures to suit my mood and feelings at the time. I do freelance/commercial work where I am adding color to another photographer's images. When doing this type of work communication between artist, art directors, etc. is most important. Another avenue which I enjoy is to copy, enlarge and handcolor very old photos.

"I have been handcoloring since 1982. I bought my first set of Marshall's Oils at a garage sale and basically just followed the directions on the enclosed leaflet, pretty much following the rules. I prefer either Agfa Portriga Rapid 118 or Oriental FBN paper; a good alternative is Kodak P Max Art RC.

"I apply photo oils with cotton swabs and loose sterilized cotton rolled into balls. I then rub down the painted area until a 'wash' of the colors I desire are achieved. I highlight or add depth to certain areas with the use of pencils and occasionally oil pastels. With certain images where I wish to show more texture, I will use sable brushes of various widths. I usually do not pre-coat the print, but where I am looking to have a smooth blending of colors, like for the sea or sky, I will use Marshall's P.M. Solution before applying the oils. Strange as it may sound, I allow the photograph to 'speak to me' about its finished look. Developing the Art of Seeing happens over time, or perhaps a lifetime."

© Karen G. Schulman

Norm Darwish

Norm Darwish is a self-taught photographer/printer whose work has appeared in numerous publications and on greeting cards, calendars and posters. He travels extensively, and sells his work at top art fairs throughout the United States. He also maintains a mailing list of current buyers, and has had much success with selling original handcolored work. His work is also in many collections, including the Michigan Artists Collection.

Says Darwish, "The pleasure in selling my work in this manner is that I can choose what I want to shoot. I am completely independent, and have no client to defer to."

Most of Darwish's images are high key, thus lend to the use of delicate colors. All his images are printed on Kodak Polyprint N surface paper. He uses TEC developer to enhance graininess.

The work is colored with a combination of Marshall's Oils and Pencils, with the pencils being used for detail work. Says Darwish, "Since I print some of the photos as small as 4x5-inches, using the pencils makes the image easier to do, and therefore affordable to the public.

"A photo that is only going to be colored with pencil will first be coated with Marshall's P.M. Solution. It is wiped on...then wiped off until you can touch the paper without making a fingerprint. I wear white cotton gloves to keep the oil from my hands off the picture, and also use them to blend the color while I work. I color many photos in a week, so have streamlined my technique."

A long-time Detroiter, Darwish recently moved to Coldwater, Michigan, where he develops, prints and handcolors his work.

© Darwish

ALLAN TEGER

"My subjects are the diners, cars, amusement parks and buildings of the 1940s and 1950s. At first I photographed such places in color, but found that the result was, for me, a simple picture of the place. It had no feeling. Using black-and-white film was better, but something was missing. Then I remembered the old hand-coloring process used for portraits long ago. That was in 1978. I tried it and found that it worked—it was the color of my memory—the timeless moment.

"I have never studied art or photography, but I hold a Ph.D in psychology. My background in psychology (especially in the psychology of consciousness and mysticism) and my practice of meditation have greatly influenced my work.

"I work with a medium format, 6x7 camera. I print on fiber-based paper and apply Marshall Photo Oils directly onto the surface of the photograph using cotton on the end of toothpicks."

Teger's work has been published extensively on cards and calendars by Pomegranate Press. His 1992 "Diner" Calendar is a classic that shows his love of an era and his hand-coloring skills.

TRACIE TAYLOR

Tracie Taylor is an accomplished photo artist represented in numerous collections throughout the country. She has an MFA in Still Photography, teaches and holds workshops for Marshall's Photo Coloring Systems.

Says Taylor, "By using Marshall's Extra Strong Oils and choosing paper with a fine-grain texture I am able to achieve the darker colors not usually associated with handcoloring. I refer to my photographs as Photo Paintings. When a lighter hue is desired I mix a ratio of one part oil with three parts Extender.

"To save time and unnecessary cleanup I predetermine what my color scheme will be by placing a sheet of tracing paper over an 8x10 print and color it with pencils. One word of caution about mixing paint: even though the oil goes a long way always mix a little more than you think you'll need. It is a good idea to work with both a daylight-corrected bulb and an incandescent light. These are the two most common light sources that the photograph will be viewed under and will help you determine how colors will appear. Avoid using fluorescent light which gives a greenish cast and distorts the color.

"By adding color you will be darkening the print so develop the print slightly lighter than normal. I also prefer to use half to one grade higher contrast than normal. A surface with fine-grained texture works best. I find matte papers too slick and difficult to work with.

"To apply oil I use a good grade of 100% cotton. Avoid using cotton with any polyester content as it does not absorb the oil. Many people use commercial cotton swabs but I prefer a smaller amount of cotton and a tighter wrap to ensure control.

"I begin by picking up paint on a cotton ball or skewer and apply it with a circular motion. The area is then carefully rubbed down, again with a circular motion, using clean cotton. With practice you learn how to lightly touch the surface and pick up just enough paint while smoothing it out. I always keep the cotton I used to rub down an area just in case I have to rework that area. When you use new cotton it picks up more than it should.

"Special care needs to be taken in removing unwanted color with Marlene Solution. Never soak the skewer. If too much Marlene is used it could bleed into adjacent areas. The oil may take a day or longer to dry, depending upon the amount of oil applied and humidity levels. Mixing the Drier directly with the oil with a 1:2 or 1:3 ratio allows the oil to dry within 24 hours."

MEHOSH DZIADZIO

Mehosh Dziadzio studied fine art under the eye of his father, who was an instructor at the Parsons School of Design in New York and Paris. He developed his photographic skills while working as an assistant to Robert Farber, a fashion and beauty photographer. His publication credits include Warner Brothers Records, ads for B.U.M. Equipment, and calendars and cards for Portal Publications. He also works as Creative Director for Photographer's Forum Magazine and California Image Sourcebook.

The image here, "Christina and the Rocket" was first created as a magazine ad for a clothing manufacturer, then reproduced as a poster. It was enlarged on Agfa Portriga Rapid Matte paper, Grade #2. Marshall's Oils were used for the overall colors, with Marshall's Pencils for details.

Says Mehosh, "I prefer to print oversize whenever possible so that the finished art 'tightens up' when reduced to reproduction size. The long grayscale of Agfa's #2 paper makes my job a lot easier. I print for the shadows, being careful not to overdevelop; that way the whites remain white and if the blacks need more punch I can go back with the oils or pencils to get the density I prefer.

"On large prints I usually start with areas at the top of the print and work my way down, so as not to smudge what I've just done. Letting each area dry down between colors is advisable. I like my colors to remain rich and vibrant, so I rub down my oils only as much as is necessary for a smooth, even tonality. The most important factor is patience. You have to take your time. Like anything, the more you do it, the easier it becomes."

GREG MACGREGOR

Greg MacGregor received his MA in Art/Photography in 1971 from San Francisco State University, and has been teaching, publishing and exhibiting his work in galleries ever since. He originated the Photography Department at California State University in Hayward, where he still teaches today. He has had over 40 one-man shows and joined in over 80 group shows. He has served as a member of the faculty at the Ansel Adams Workshop and published "The California Emigrant Trail, 1840-1860" with the University of New Mexico Press .

Says MacGregor, "The reason I began hand-coloring in 1976 was in response to the new acceptance of color photography in the commercial gallery world. I was convinced that the rapid color fading properties of prints would lead to a quick collapse of interest. I was wrong; however, it was clear that for the first time, buyers and collectors were interested in color. I wanted something permanent.

"My first series, titled "Remains", began in 1976 and continues today. It began as a science fiction series of landscapes using the American desert as raw material. It now incorporates a notion of dead technology as if civilization used to live here and vanished. The choice of hand-painting worked with this series because I could choose non-realistic color, which supported the theme.

"The second major series, begun in 1980, is titled 'New Woman of the American West'. It began as a comment on the return of materialism and feminine glamour into American culture. Here I want bright, 'happy-Hollywood' type colors to emphasize the point. My intended market for these was the newly-emerging greeting card business which was using pop-culture material (compared to decades of flowers and pets) for images."

MacGregor says his techniques with Marshall Oils are fairly "standard", using cotton balls to apply color and blend in larger areas, and cotton swabs for smaller areas. Marshall's pencils are used for detail work.

Says MacGregor, "The most problematical area for me are the sky blends. Western skys are often cloudless blue, which translates as gray on black-and-white film. I tone my prints to an off-shade of brown (with various toners) but it still remains a difficult job. My solution is to build color density by applying several coats of color, letting each color dry before applying the next."

Another problem area MacGregor has solved is dust attaching itself to the print surface during drydown. He shares his solution: "I dry prints inside a plastic bag sealed shut on the ends with a cardboard 'bridge' inside to keep the plastic from touching the print."

Six Gun Spin at Rio Grande Gorge © G. MacGregor 1991, from "New Woman of the America West" series

Goblin Valley Starfield © G. MacGregor, 1976

RITA DIBERT

Rita Dibert received her Master of Fine Arts from the University of Michigan in 1971. She has been involved with teaching for many years, including five years as Assistant Professor of Art at Hartwick College in Oneonta, NY. She also was an Artist in Residence and Assistant Professor of Art at Pomona College, Claremont, CA. Most recently, she has been working as a Lecturer in Electronic Media and Photography at the University of North Carolina at Charlotte. She has been associated with the Xochipilli Gallery in Birmingham, MI, since 1970.

Dibert's work is in numerous corporate and museum collections, including Polaroid Corp., Upjohn Corporation, the Detroit Institute of Art and the Museum of Photography, Riverside, CA.

She has received numerous grants and awards, and has been in many one-person and group shows. She has also curated exhibits on Hand Manipulated Photography.

Says Dibert, "I utilize Marshall's Oils to enable me to control color completely, and have done so since 1975. I prefer to tint on fiber-based, warm-toned papers such as Portriga Rapid or Oriental; I selenium tone and air dry these prints. I apply the colors with hand-rolled cotton swabs, and utilize over 40 years of painting experience to mix colors.

"I tint on regular panchromatic film images, as well as Polaroid 55 N/P, but prefer to work on infrared film."

JO WHALEY

Jo Whaley has both an M.F.A in Art and an M.A. in Photography from the University of California, Berkeley. Her work is in numerous public and private collections, including the San Francisco Museum of Modern Art and the BankAmerica Corporation Art Collection. She has exhibited in numerous one person and group shows throughout the eighties and nineties, including shows at the Sante Fe Museum of Fine Arts, the University Art Museum in Albuquerque, NM, the Tortino Fotographia Biennale, Italy and at the Scheinbaum and Russek Gallery in Sante Fe.

Whaley's work has taken many directions, two of which are shown here. One is a series called "Shrines" (top image), handcolored black-and-white photographs incorporated into mixed media sculptures. Says Whaley, "The reference in both the titles and the architectural form is to that of religious shrines, particularly those of early and primitive Catholicism. Traditionally, those who have attained an unearthly form of perfection are the subjects of shrines. I, however, enshrine the more humble aspects of the human condition...I enshrine such common states as melancholy, frivolity, vanity and boredom."

The images are assembled using arched wooden boxes in which Whaley incorporates various materials. These are "temporary sculptural installations" which she photographs with a view camera. Says Whaley, "The resulting photographs are then handcolored in an expressive rather than a representational manner."

Whaley's "Santos" series (bottom) displays one of the most unique uses of Marshall's Photo Oils. These are color matte-surface prints which she collages, then applies Marshall's Oils with cotton and brushes. Says Whaley, "After tinting the photo with oil I set it with steam, then do the brushwork.

"I find that painting in layers, allowing each layer to dry in the manner of the old master glazing techniques, is most effective where richness and subtlety is desired. After these layers have dried, going in with brushwork adds dimension.

"To clean edges or remove unwanted paint from small areas a kneaded eraser is terrific. It can be molded to any shape, is self-cleaning and does not leave crumbs. I have also built little drying boxes so that the prints can air dry free from dust."

© Jo Whaley, 1984

© Jo Whaley, 1990

Richard Prehn

Richard Prehn began photographing in 1971, and has studied and practiced the art of handcoloring for over 17 years. He served as a stringer for United Press International (UPI) for ten years, and he has also worked for Associated Press and the Reuters news agencies. Along with his work in photo art, he works in a wide range of fields, including commercial, architectural, glamour and forensic photography. He has been published widely, and has exhibited his work in the United States and overseas. In 1989, at the invitation of the Cultural Minister of the Soviet Union, he presented a photographic exhibit there, where he also taught seminars in photography and photo oil techniques. He has also had his work published for use on calendars and posters.

Prehn's handcoloring work is extremely diverse—the two presented here are but samples of his wide-ranging styles. He prints on Kodak Ektalure paper and, for certain images, prints on the dark side for what he describes as a "somber effect." The image on the lower right shows his heavy oil technique.

Says Prehn, "When I load a skewer to do heavy oils like this I work it like a palette knife or full brush. I control the densities with the thickness of the paint. On some occasions, I clean out certain areas to emphasize a part of the picture."

For the still life, some of his skewers were loaded with four colors. "As the colors were applied I turned the skewer to create the effect. Each stroke is left in a picture like this, not smoothed. As the next stroke is applied the color is blended into the color previously applied."

Prehn notes that the heavy oils certainly take longer to dry than the lighter oil applications.

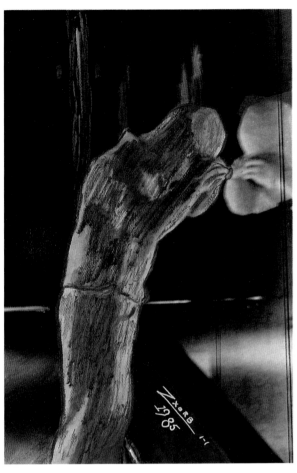

Artists' Directory

Paula Boam
703 No. Beverly Drive
Beverly Hills, CA 90210

Terence A. Chua
32768 Hanford Court
Union City, CA 94587-5601

Sandra Russell Clark
906 Esplanade Avenue C
New Orleans, LA 70116

Colortone Artists
Pat Smith, Proprietor & Colorist
Elsie Moltz, Colorist
6812 North Clark Street
Chicago, IL 60626

Norm Darwish
298 West Chicago
Coldwater, MI 49036

Mehosh Dziadzio
PO Box 20106
Santa Barbara, CA 93101
805 966-2332

Rita Dibert
Art Department
University of North Carolina at Charlotte
Charlotte, NC 28223
704 547-2473

Jill Enfield
211 East 18th Street
New York City, NY 10003

Rena Bass Forman
744 River Road
Piermont, NY 10968

Kathleen Francour
Photographic Artist
16161 Ventura Blvd. Suite#767
Encino, CA 91436-1315
818 907-5421 FAX:818 907-5238

Michael Gesinger
17511 88th Avenue NE
Bothell, WA 98011

Deborah Gilbert
16 W 16th Street, #14JS
New York City, NY 10011

Marsha Polier-Grossman
14509 Standing Oak Court
Midlothian, VA 23113
804-739-0717 (home/studio)

Nora Hernandez
Bonnets & Lace
1940 Corbett Highlands Place
Arroyo Grande, CA 93420

Colleen Kenyon
Route 212
Shady, NY 12409

Lawson P. (Phillip & Pamela)
8809 Oakwilde Lane
Los Angeles, CA 90046

Barbara E. Leven
25-19 30th Drive, #1N
Astoria, NY 11102
718 204-7250

Peggy Lindt
1627 Calle Canon
Santa Barbara, CA 93101
Phone/FAX: 805 569-1002

Greg MacGregor
6481 Colby Street
Oakland, CA 94618
510 658-8331

Jennifer J. McClintock
5431 Lake Murray Blvd. #6
La Mesa, CA 91942